Powering Through Pressure

PEARSON

At Pearson, we believe in learning – all kinds of learning for all kinds of people. Whether it's at home, in the classroom or in the workplace, learning is the key to improving our life chances.

That's why we're working with leading authors to bring you the latest thinking and best practices, so you can get better at the things that are important to you. You can learn on the page or on the move, and with content that's always crafted to help you understand quickly and apply what you've learned.

If you want to upgrade your personal skills or accelerate your career, become a more effective leader or more powerful communicator, discover new opportunities or simply find more inspiration, we can help you make progress in your work and life.

Pearson is the world's leading learning company. Our portfolio includes the Financial Times and our education business, Pearson International.

Every day our work helps learning flourish, and wherever learning flourishes, so do people.

To learn more, please visit us at **www.pearson.com/uk**

Powering Through Pressure

Building resilience for when work gets tough

Bruce Hoverd

Harlow, England • London • New York • Boston • San Francisco • Toronto • Sydney • Auckland • Singapore • Hong Kong
Tokyo • Seoul • Taipei • New Delhi • Cape Town • São Paulo • Mexico City • Madrid • Amsterdam • Munich • Paris • Milan

PEARSON EDUCATION LIMITED

Edinburgh Gate
Harlow CM20 2JE
United Kingdom
Tel: +44 (0)1279 623623
Website: www.pearson.com/uk

First published 2014 (print and electronic)

Pearson Education is not responsible for the content of third-party internet sites.

ISBN: 978–1-292–00476–1 (print)
      978–1-292–00863–9 (PDF)
      978–1-292–00809–7 (eText)
      978–1-292–00864–6 (ePub)

British Library Cataloguing-in-Publication Data
A catalogue record for the print edition is available from the British Library

Library of Congress Cataloguing-in-Publication Data
Hoverd, Bruce.
  Powering through pressure : building resilience for when work gets tough / Bruce Hoverd. – One Edition.
      pages cm
  Includes bibliographical references and index.
  ISBN 978-1-292-00476-1 (print) – ISBN 978-1-292-00863-9 (PDF) – ISBN 978-1-292-00809-7 (eText) – ISBN 978-1-292-00864-6 (ePub)
  1. Job stress--Prevention. 2. Resilience (Personality trait) 3. Time management. I. Title.
  HF5548.85.H6748 2014
  158.7'2--dc23
                                        2013051023

10 9 8 7 6 5 4 3 2 1
18 17 16 15 14

Text design by Design Deluxe
Cover design by David Eldridge
Print edition typeset in Helvetica Neue LT Pro in 9pt by 3

Print edition printed and bound in Great Britain by Henry Ling Ltd., at the Dorset Press, Dorchester, Dorset.

Note that any page cross references refer to the print edition

Contents

Publisher's acknowledgements

We are grateful to the following for permission to reproduce copyright material:

Franklin Covey Co. for permission to reproduce figure on page 26, adapted from Stephen Covey, *The Seven Habits of Highly Effective People*, Schuster 1994. Jeff Archer, www.the-tonic.com, for permission to reproduce the figure on page 42. Scribner Publishing Group and Taylor & Francis Books (UK) for figure on page 88, adapted from Kübler-Ross, *On Death and Dying*, Routledge 1969. Copyright © 1969 by Elisabeth Kübler-Ross, copyright renewed © 1997 by Elisabeth Kübler-Ross; all rights reserved.

Illustrations courtesy of Shutterstock: p.14 arka38; p.31 Konstantinos Kokkinis; p.51 Dr.G; p.68 Borislav Bajkic; p.83 MarijaPiliponyte; p.98 Cartoonresource; p.114 tibori; p.130 iQoncept; p.133 Cycloneproject; p.136 diez artwork; p.139 RetroClipArt; p.141 donskarpo; p.143 the adam design studio; p.145 Nowik Sylwia; p.147 Scott Richardson; p.150 Kudryashka; p.153 art4all; p.156 Memo Angeles; p.158 SiwaBudda; p.161 ottoflick.

In some instances we have been unable to trace the owners of copyright material and we would appreciate any information that would enable us to do so.

About the author

Bruce Hoverd was born, and spent his formative years, in New Zealand. After a human resources career within four large, but very different organisations, he has worked as a consultant and coach with hundreds of businesses for 20 years. He is now the managing director of Managing Pressure Limited, working with individuals and organisations to reduce stress, control pressure and build resilience. His work has included initiatives throughout Europe, the Middle East, Africa and Asia.

Introduction

My stress breakthrough realisation

A moment of enlightenment for me, concerning what stress was about, occurred when I was working late in the company offices one evening. I was about to leave the building when a strange sound, coming from one of the few, lit offices, immediately attracted my attention. I peered in and was terrified by what I saw. A colleague I knew well was rocking back-and-forth, crying out like a wild animal. After taking action to ensure that he received appropriate immediate support, I was left with the question, how had he got to this state without our recognising the pressure he was under? This led me to ask what we could have done to prevent this dignified, competent person ever reaching this point of distress.

In our workplaces, homes and social gathering points, there are people who need us to answer this question and to take the necessary actions to ensure that they will be supported appropriately. This desire to spread the word about recognising pressure points and providing early support became the mission for me and my company. I want to create the means by which as many people as possible take those early actions that will reduce pressure and prevent the common decline into unnecessary stress. From this and many other experiences I have learnt that breaking the unhealthy stress cycle is possible. The good news is that, by increasing your awareness, responding early and maintaining small changes, you can lead a stress-free life. It's about the choices you make, the options you explore and the support you are willing to give and seek.

What will make the real difference? There is no magic pill, just your increased ability to think about pressure in different ways and do things differently, on a daily basis, to reduce demands, retain energy and remain healthy. Preventing stress becomes easier if you recognise how many alternatives you have available and you are willing to make clear decisions that will support how you want to positively and optimistically live and work.

My aim in writing this book is to help you to recognise what you need to do when you are faced by increasing levels of pressure. Pulling together my thoughts and the ideas drawn from the experience of thousands of my colleagues and clients, you will be introduced to and reminded about a wide range of positive actions and solutions to prevent stress. You will discover that some of these will work for you to reduce demands, deal with the underlying causes and enable you to become more aware of the signs of growing pressure.

Chapter One describes the way that you and others **tread the challenge and stress path**. I have provided a way for you to identify how serious the pressure is that you face, how to recognise your own particular patterns in reacting to this pressure, and what type of support you will need, at a given point. Once you recognise the effect of your responses to the demands and challenges you encounter, you will understand the importance of taking appropriate action.

In Chapter Two you can explore one of the major challenges that sits at the heart of rising levels of pressure for many people. How often do you experience that over-riding sense of having **too much to do and not enough time?** Resolving this dilemma first involves recognising where your time demons lie and then having a range of alternative strategies to make the best use of the time you have available.

Most of us rely on our favourite tactics to get us through the week and to remain sane and healthy enough to enjoy the weekend. In Chapter Three **developing coping tactics that work**, I ask you to question whether your current approaches merely delay the obvious, and do not deal with the issues you face. Are you making use of the wide range of activities and responses that could recharge your batteries? Chapter Three examines what you can do both within the workplace, and outside, to top up your energy reservoir regularly and provide sufficient strength when you most need a resilient state.

Chapter Four highlights the difference in pressure that is generated by the way we think about, approach and deal with 'difficult' situations. There may be many circumstances that you do not find easy to manage on a daily basis, but you can reduce your daily pressure by **thinking about negative situations in different ways**. The ideas presented will enable you to develop flexibility in your approach and response, ultimately helping you to avoid conflict, remain calm and be able to deal with and resolve issues, at their source.

Chapter Five allows you to consider how problems with your relationships add to the pressures you face at work and outside. By introducing some ways of understanding these situations, and suggesting the means to develop alternative strategies for managing them, you will be able to reduce pressure points dramatically. **Addressing relationships that aren't working** will allow you to have greater energy, a more positive attitude, and the personal optimism needed to achieve what you value and think is important.

Feeling good about change is something we want to have but more often the real experience produces fear, anxiety and uncertainty. In Chapter Six I challenge the assumption that change has to be difficult, and look at some ways that you can make change work for yourself and others around you.

Exploring the level and provision of support you will need to handle pressure, by continuously **developing the support networks you need** is the theme of Chapter Seven. Unless you consciously put work into building and sustaining the appropriate support network, there will be few places to go when the pressure really ramps up. It is also essential to understand what professional support is out there for you and your colleagues to draw upon, as issues arise and challenges take their toll.

Chapter Eight takes each of the six main elements within our model of **building your personal resilience** and identifies ways of strengthening these, so that you will have the right resources to deal more effectively with constant change, tough times and setbacks. I will demonstrate that if you can develop all these areas of resilience, you can stop stress at its source. The ability to bounce back from setbacks is one of the most critical life and work skills.

Finally, in Chapter Nine I have attached a theme connected with pressure that each month might represent for you. You will find thought-provoking suggestions and ideas that you can adopt to help you to sustain and win your battle with conquering stress. **Reducing pressure throughout the year** supports my principle idea that tackling difficulties and concerns on a regular basis is the best way of releasing and controlling pressure.

You will have deduced from the title and this introduction that I absolutely believe that it is within your power to prevent stress, by harnessing all the resources you have available, when you start to come under pressure. It is therefore not the difficult situations you face that count, it is your response to these circumstances and the anxiety accompanying your actions that matters in your stopping stress in its tracks. These elements are within your control and I have set out to provide a whole range of options that will increase your chances of strengthening your response and behaviour.

Now it is up to you to find the ideas that are personally meaningful and action these to create your own stress-free zone ...

Treading the challenge and stress path

Chapter One

> **I try not to listen to the shoulds or coulds, and try to get beyond expectations, peer pressure, or trying to please – and just listen. I believe that all the anwers are ultimately within us.** KIM CATTRALL

Our business lives are becoming more and more pressurised. We're so caught up in the frenetic pace, with higher levels of demand and more resource constraints, that we don't recognise when the pressure becomes too much. Or, worse still, we ignore it.

So a good place to start on your pressure journey is by developing the ability, at any point, to recognise where you are with the demands you face. This will prompt a greater desire for you to look after yourself and will provide you with an increased awareness of the clues and actions needed for you to move into and remain in a healthier state.

First I ask you to consider this model that best summarises this process.

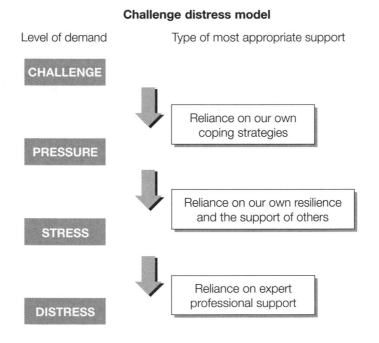

Challenge distress model

Level of demand | Type of most appropriate support

CHALLENGE

Reliance on our own coping strategies

PRESSURE

Reliance on our own resilience and the support of others

STRESS

Reliance on expert professional support

DISTRESS

This is the state I want you to hold in your mind as the point you can get to that will indicate that you have been successful in reducing pressure and preventing stress.

My fundamental belief is that the more we learn from the positive ways we have lived our lives, the ways that have helped us to remain in an enlightened, healthy state, the greater the chance that we will experience periods free of strong challenge, high pressure, stress and distress. Your first starting point, therefore, in preventing stress and distress, is realising what has enabled you to be healthy, fit, resilient and well, then set out to create as many opportunities as you can to recapture these experiences.

Activity

Ask yourself these questions and remind yourself what you did to create or contribute to the healthy position you were in:

When in my life was I at my most fit?
When did I feel healthiest?
At which times have I had the highest energy levels?
When did I bounce back from difficult situations?
What do I do that enables me to feel most positive and optimistic?

It's quite likely (given that you're reading this) that your answer to these questions is not **now**. But if you adapt, those odd rare moments that you treasure and draw positive energy from, can then become 'the norm'.

Now you are ready to explore the different levels outlined in the model given.

The challenge level

For most, challenge is the normal state of our working lives, where we 'just get on with it'. We can even derive some energy, satisfaction and motivation from having tasks that stretch us, time constraints that push us, and issues to resolve that extend us.

Acceptance that this is the norm can be very healthy, helping us realistically to recognise what we can influence and change, but there is nearly always a downside. Continuous periods of challenge lead to serious wear and tear, which is likely to deplete our overall energy levels, weaken our immune systems and reduce our ability to cope.

Maintaining a high, recurring level of active response to deal with a series of demands means that our physical, mental and emotional systems frequently are on alert. This increases the chance of putting a strain on all our available resources. Imagine yourself holding things in place, like a stretch band that is constantly straining. People often describe this state as tense, taut and stretched. The personal effect of being in this position is usually less time for relaxation, fewer opportunities for recharging your batteries and a growing sense of there being less respite.

How do you know when challenge is beginning to affect you? Here are six of the most common indicators:

→ Difficulty in getting to sleep and waking feeling unrefreshed.
→ More tiredness than usual.
→ Emotions that feel close to the surface.
→ Difficulty focusing on tasks at hand.
→ Low energy at particular times of day.
→ Impatience or frustration, which is evident in your response to others.

To put the brakes on your likely descent into the pressure zone, you will need to:

→ find ways of reducing your workload through delegating tasks or asking for support;
→ introduce a method of relaxation that works for you, such as meditation, so you can switch off from work;
→ develop a sleep routine, so you are better rested;
→ take more breaks, timeout or organise a holiday;
→ seek out people who will recharge your batteries and help you get a different or more positive perspective on your situation;

Powering Through Pressure

→ eat in a balanced way and undertake activity to balance your energy levels.

Also you will need to be aware that, when you are challenged, you are likely to affect the state of others around you. It is helpful to notice when you get more abrupt responses, start to experience tension in your interactions and encounter others switching off. These signs normally mean that your pressure is in some way becoming infectious, or others are feeling dumped upon. These first signs are very good orange light indicators. They normally signal 'proceed with caution, it is time to check out what's happening!' Slow down! Do something different.

The pressure level

If you haven't been able to find and use ways of managing your challenging situation, you probably will experience different aspects of your state beginning to deteriorate. This means you are in the pressure zone. The easiest way of knowing if this is happening to you, is for you to identify whether you are showing an increasing number of signs and symptoms. If so, this will indicate that you are finding it less easy to deal with the demands and anxieties of your work.

It is essential at this time that you bring out your favourite coping strategies and use them more often to get you through increasingly difficult days and weeks. This is the only way that you will remain healthy and sane. Choosing the most appropriate strategies is explored in more detail in Chapter Three.

Remember, how you choose to respond to this growing pressure will influence dramatically the route that you ultimately take.

Based on our research, we have established that there are three common ways that people respond at the stage of pressure. Which of these responses do you hear yourself making?

The stubborn and bloody-minded 'rhino' type response:

→ 'I just need to keep on going';
→ 'I don't do stress';
→ 'What pressure?';
→ 'I must work harder'.

The mindless and ignorant 'ostrich' type response:

→ 'It will go away';
→ 'This is no big deal, it's not an issue';
→ 'Stress is for wimps'.

The self-aware and enlightened 'evolved' response:

→ 'This is not right and I need to do something about it';
→ 'It's time I made some changes'.

How observant and aware are you of the growing number of key signs that signal that your pressure is increasing? The most reliable indicators can occur in three areas.

Your physical state:

→ headaches;
→ a series of colds;
→ growing aches, pains or soreness in your joints, especially neck and backache;
→ tired eyes;
→ low energy;
→ excessive tiredness;
→ difficulty remaining asleep;
→ skin eruptions that stay.

Your body is telling you it is in some way aching from being put under strain.

Your emotional/relationship state:

→ changing moods;
→ anger;
→ irrational reactions;
→ strong emotional reactions to minor irritants;
→ intolerance;
→ complaining about anything and everything.

Your emotions are telling you that you are not responding in your normal confident way.

Your thinking state:

→ forgetfulness of important things;

→ mistakes in areas where normally you would be accurate or meticulous;

→ loss of focus and distraction during tasks, meetings or presentations;

→ demotivation;

→ more incomplete tasks than is usual;

→ loss of confidence.

Your brain and nervous system are telling you that the links are not operating smoothly and could become short-circuited.

You may have experienced all of these symptoms at some stage, but a warning sign is critical when you have a lot of them at once and you become very different to your 'normal' state – this is pressure!

Personal case study

To illustrate this, I want to share the experience of my client Rob, who had a very common pressure pattern that you may well recognise in your position. He was a newly promoted petrochemicals manager, in his early thirties. When we met he had not made the links consciously between various aspects of his current situation or recognised that changing one element may have an effect on the other elements of his situation. I was struck immediately by how many warning signs he described. He talked about his current work position and listed an assortment of challenges that he was facing ...

As you might conclude, seeing the full picture showed him the extent of his issues and the dangers of not taking action to prevent worsening problems. And the good news was: first, the more he talked about his situation, the more he recognised that the way he was dealing with his position was not working, and he could not continue with his current approach and inaction. He even said that he thought he had buried his head in the sand.

Second, he agreed that he needed to make some quite big changes and take some immediate actions.

▶

Typical Pressure Cycle

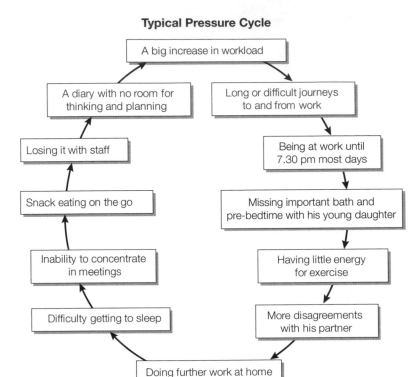

Third, he recognised that he was in control of his state and he could deal with the issues that he was facing.

Finally, he accepted that he needed some support from others to really bring about relief. For a strong, fit guy, asking for help was not easy.

We discussed his cycle of negative health symptoms and how they were linked. He identified the most important issues and explored the causes that were driving his situation. As a result, he agreed to make five important changes:

1   He would delegate and let go of some of the tasks that he now acknowledged were really part of his old job. These he had held onto because he enjoyed doing them, rather than needing to be involved.
2   The family would move to a house that was much closer to his workplace. This would remove difficult journeys and allow more time at home.
3   An agreement was made, with a group of his close peers, that the first person to leave the office each day would contact the others and they would all then do what was needed to close down and leave within 15 minutes. All of them recognised they had developed an unhelpful pattern that they could break more easily, through collective action.

4   No work would be done after 8.30 pm, and he would be unavailable by mobile or email at weekends.
5   A standard booking was set up for two months to play tennis twice a week, close to his workplace with three of his friends. This was agreed and implemented immediately.

What struck me most was the committed optimism he demonstrated whilst remaining realistic about what was achievable with his goals. Attached to each of these important changes were specific targets that were stretching and sustainable. This fitted with his preference for learning, based on taking on new challenges. He could also get some quick wins and make incremental gains that would encourage him to keep going.

Three months later, the energetic, bright faced, younger-looking man who strode purposefully into my office was unrecognisable from the person I had first encountered.

Activity

Ask yourself these questions:

How much of Rob's situation is reflected in your life?
What does his story suggest to you that is worth you considering and making changes right now?

The stress level

We define stress as the state where our own resources are proving insufficient to deal or cope with the growing, often continuous, demands that we are facing. So, having relied on all the things we do daily, to manage or contain the pressures we are facing, our coping strategies are no longer enough. The resultant effect is that a number of the signs of pressure now have become more regular, frequent patterns, and are having a stronger impact on our state. This is recognised often by others, before we accept what is happening.

At this stage, almost certainly we require support from others to achieve relief, make changes or drive through improvements to our state of health. Too many people battle on, thinking they have to deal with everything stressful that is occurring, by themselves. There is only one result from this response and that is an increase in unresolved issues, greater inability to cope and more ineffective responses to the situations we face.

At a stress level, clearly you will notice and be affected by some of these red flag warnings and patterns:

→ headaches that have become migraines;

→ a series of colds that develop into influenza or bronchitis;

→ occasional back strain that has now deteriorated into near-permanent, incapacitating backaches, causing constant discomfort;

→ irritation and frustration that has evolved into streams of angry outbursts;

→ unsociability that has reached a point of dramatic withdrawal;

→ tiredness that now means you have very low energy, most of the time;

→ forgetfulness that is now evident in you making major errors or poor decisions;

→ sadness that leaves you sunk into periods of loneliness and feeling depressed;

→ lowered self-esteem that now generates a sense of hopelessness;

→ mood swings that now are experienced by others as 'losing it'.

Considering some examples of stress indicators that I encounter with clients and that commonly you might observe, will help you to identify where there are changes to the signs and symptoms. They will also be evidence of alterations to responses in the face of growing demands across the four levels of stress. These typically changing patterns are:

Challenge	Pressure	Stress	Distress
Muscle tightening	Headaches	Migraines	Blackout
Butterflies	Nausea	Diarrhoea	IBS
Impatience	Irritability	Aggression	Violence
Quietness	Withdrawal	Avoidance	Isolation
Intense concentration	Losing focus	Inattention	Memory loss
Questioning	Self-doubt	Sadness	Depression
Erratic sleep	Waking unrefreshed	Restlessness	Insomnia

Powering Through Pressure

Hopefully you can see easily the serious effect of these combined stress indicators. Stress is not a label attached to everyday ailments or something to be used as an excuse to take time out. When this level is really experienced, our bodies are screaming out in ways we must take notice of. And still some people carry on in pain, not getting the help they need and being unable to function effectively. Often they have had years of practice and the unacceptable situation has become the norm.

The distress level

What none of us want to find ourselves experiencing is the level of distress. This is the point where problems have worsened to become chronic, long-term and debilitating. You will have reached this point only if you have not taken action at an earlier stage and not been able to access the support that is available. By this stage, you will have become almost totally reliant on expert and professional help to deal with the serious mental, emotional and physical issues you face. It is others, hopefully, who will lead us on the road to some form of recovery.

We are all aware of examples of others, if not ourselves, where life has become a fight to survive. Far too common examples include depression, pneumonia, serious ongoing heart issues, recurrent insomnia preventing recovery, shutdown and withdrawal, inability to move about, eating disorders, and disturbing patterns and responses when dealing with others.

In the workplace, managers and colleagues must do what they can to help people who are returning to work after suffering from a distressed condition. You can play a critical role by ensuring that people who have been on longer-term sick leave are doing only what they are capable of, without further pressure. That means removing issues that may have affected their health in the first place. For those who have been in this position, this support from colleagues on their return is an essential part of their recovery.

If you need convincing that stress and pressure are relevant issues in all workplaces and that you have a role to play in reducing them, it may be helpful to understand and be aware of some of the causes and costs of stress.

It is not enough to recognise the signs of stress, if we are to really make progress and regain health. We need to identify the sources of pressure coming from different areas of our lives, which have contributed to a stressful state. Some of these we can have some control or influence over and, as a result, take conscious actions. Others are things that have just happened, outside of our control, and the secret with these is to learn to change or adapt our response to them.

Look at some of the causative factors that we have helped people to resolve and identify–which of these might be relevant to you and your situation? These lists are not intended to cover every single thing and may well prompt you to identify other issues that are affecting you.

Work

Job pressures and targets

Boss – their style and behaviour

Employees – their attitude and behaviour

Colleagues – relationships with them

Communication – or lack of

Lack of direction or goals

Lack of control over job

Work environment

Lack of support or training

Pressure to work long hours

Culture

Bullying

Changes to job

Threat of losing your job

Family/relationships

Problems in key relationship – arguing or not communicating

Arguments with children

Arguments with parents

Need to care for a family member (especially long term)

Serious illness within the family

Concerns about behaviour of close family member

Dealing with an ex-partner or spouse

Dealing with stepchildren or partner's children

No personal time or space

Death within the family

Environmental

Home location

Neighbours

Moving house

Self–lifestyle

Ambitions and aspiration

Financial pressures to maintain lifestyle

Travel, especially commuting	Debt worries
Crowded environment	Personal relationships
Noise	Keeping up with friends
Pollution of other sorts	Peer group
Threat (e.g. concerns about violence or crime)	Social life

General

Lack of fitness

Diet

Smoking and/or drinking

No time for self

No relaxation time

In the longer term, only by addressing what is causing the pressure will you and others be able to achieve a healthy state that is stress free. Everyone has a role to play in reducing pressured conditions that result in the considerable consequences and costs I have outlined.

I remember a night lying in a critical condition in our local hospital and look back with horror at myself for not having taken action soon enough and dealt with the issues. The evolving signs were there and I failed to listen to others' warnings.

I have fully recovered now, but I do not want you to find yourself in a similar position.

Remember

Stress affects one in five of the working population, from the newest recruit in the post room to the board of directors.

Stress is now the single biggest cause of sickness in the UK.

Over 105 million days are lost to stress each year – costing UK employers £1.24 billion.

Source: Health & Safety Executive

Summary

In this chapter you will have considered where you currently find yourself on the challenge-pressure-stress-distress framework. This will enable you to consider what self-help you can bring or where you need the support of others.

The four key points about recognition of the stress path and call to action are:

→ Recognise your state before the pressure becomes too great to deal with on your own.

→ Make small and easy changes as soon as you get orange light signs of pressure.

→ You have an important role in supporting others who are experiencing pressure. Become aware of the signs that are likely to indicate this.

→ It is essential to be able to ask for and offer help and support, as a major part of reducing pressure at work and outside work.

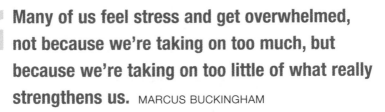

Many of us feel stress and get overwhelmed, not because we're taking on too much, but because we're taking on too little of what really strengthens us. MARCUS BUCKINGHAM

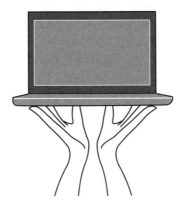

Too much to do and not enough time

Chapter Two

Time is the coin of your life. It is the only coin you have, and only you can determine how it will be spent. Be careful lest you let other people spend it for you. CARL SANDBURG

When we ask people what the biggest issue they face at work is, that puts pressure on them, and drains their energy, they usually reply, 'We have too much to do in too little time.' This often can be a direct result of a reduction in staff numbers, shorter timescales and a culture that is becoming dominated by expectations of instant responses. In businesses where the employees fear negative repercussions and reactions from their bosses and managers, many will not tackle this issue. Yet I know of very few people who have been disciplined or laid off for saying no, let alone having a discussion with their boss about what is possible. Even in our current economic climate, the worst that can happen is that people will insist that you do what they are demanding of you, or asking for. Remember, in all situations, you have a choice about how you respond to these demands.

Imagine a typical day, when you have a series of meetings, emails and calls, during which you collect more activities and tasks to do. These are in addition to the ones you have planned for, and you've probably not had time to do those either. Given this familiar pattern, it is not surprising that many people struggle to complete this ever-growing set of activities and projects. The effect of this process is that more people end up taking work home on a regular basis, frequently stay later and often hurry to complete tasks. It also leads to one of the other biggest complaints that we hear, a tendency to 'overpromise and under-deliver'.

Recently, I discovered some work by Simon Collinson, Professor of International Business at Henley Business School focussing on turning complexity into simplicity. I *used my version of this* with a management group who realised they needed to take collective action to improve their self-management and reduce their personal health risk. His tongue-in-cheek thoughts helped them to realise how ridiculous yet habit-forming some of their approaches to self-management were. Based on this work, consider the areas that may be wasting your working day. These could include:

Powering Through Pressure

→ working really hard but going in the wrong direction, especially doing activities that have little impact on the value-driven elements of your part of the business;

→ being an expert at everything and trying to do everything yourself;

→ 'analysis paralysis' – carrying out too much research and analysis on an issue or project, until you have so much information that you are unable to make a decision and, as a result, you incur delays;

→ over-intellectualising and over-complicating everything you can, especially by focussing on the politics and avoiding the truth and taking action;

→ involving everyone in everything, including those who are unable to add to the discussion, or are not affected by it;

→ ensuring that you keep working at something until you get 100 per cent of every task right, every time, to cover all the bases, and produce perfect results;

→ reinventing the wheel by changing all that comes across your desk or via email;

→ making email the focus of your entire day and ensuring you respond immediately to the humorous and unimportant ones. Not bothering to use the phone or meeting face-to-face with those situated close to you;

→ duplicating by doing someone else's work and allocating the same amount of time to every task;

→ having '250' projects, all running at the same time, in which you have a major involvement or are leading.

Activity

Do you recognise any or all of these elements in your working week, which are adding to the pressure and demands you face? These are usually self-inflicted, so you can start changing the way you use your time now by asking yourself:

Am I doing the right things?

Am I doing things in the best way?

Am I operating to an informal set of rules? (Where no one has ever told me, 'This is the way it has to be done,' but I am following this route anyway.)

Hopefully by now you will have concluded that some of the usual methods you use for tackling a heavy workload may only be adding to the pressure or shifting it into another area of your life. What can you do that will make a difference?

In response to the areas that my clients have identified as self-management issues, I have compiled the following list.

Top 10 ways of reducing time and resource pressures

1 Always begin the week, and day, with a plan that you track and refer back to

Plans are designed to help people to stay focussed, remain on track, and be aware of what needs doing at any point. At the same time, any planning process needs to allow for interruptions, changes and additional demands. You will gain an enormous amount by practising a form of flexible planning with built-in time for reflection. As you go, adjust your plan and update it.

It is also self-defeating to schedule back-to-back meetings. I often encounter people who have rushed breathless from one meeting, are still thinking about actions they need to take, and have done little preparation for the situation they are about to enter. How can they expect to contribute fully? How can being in this state allow you to be a competent, influential and effective professional?

The best plans are also based on well-formed outcomes, which describe the specific **outputs**, **decisions** and **responses** that you want to achieve. If these are clear, then you will always have a focus and be aware how close you are to achieving success. Evaluating what you have achieved around the middle of the day will allow you to make changes, reschedule activities, re-prioritise and decide what further support you need to get. At any point you need to be able to explain your well-formed outcomes, so that others are more aware of your focus and priorities, and how it will impact on them.

Using a disciplined approach will increase the chances of your doing what you hope to, in order to stay fitter, healthier and energised. It only takes 5 minutes!

PLANNING WHAT YOUR IDEAL DAY WILL BE LIKE

Consider specific times throughout the day when you want to carry out your healthy living, fitness and well-being activities:	Specify what is important for you to do, with whom and anything you want to gain from it:
At home before travel leave home by 07.45	Check arrangements finalised for school trip
Mid-morning 10.30	Coffee meeting with project colleagues, are they ok with new schedule?
Lunchtime 12.30	Walk to shops and collect soup lunch
Mid-afternoon	Fruit and nuts around team! Who will be at presentation?
Evening 18.00	Squash team ladder match at home courts
Night/pre-bed Early night!	Book theatre for Thursday

Source: based on work by Jeff Archer, www.the-tonic.com

Some people find it useful to complete their planning for a whole week, so that they are more likely to prioritise and link their well-being activities. Others complete daily, some at the end of the day, to enable them to close down the day and make arrangements for the next one.

Some of the areas that you can consider including in your plan are:

→ Travel plans and arrangements, allowing sufficient timing to avoid rushing from one place to another and ensuring you arrive in a fit state.

→ Family commitments, making sure that you are there for those things that matter to you and others.

→ Thinking about nutritional balance, so that you can maintain energy throughout the day and are shopping to stock the foods that will energise you and your family.

→ Social arrangements, where you want to make commitments and bookings for activities and events that will enable you to spend time with the people who matter, you can have fun and who energise you.

→ Sporting and fitness activities, planned for regularity, to keep your health plans on track.

This overall plan can be then be broken down into daily activity plans.

Personal case study

I have reproduced part of a revised day plan that was created by Jan, a call centre team leader. She had hugely overloaded her days and dramatically short-changed her own needs, during the months prior to my working with her.

Day 2	Outcomes	Timing	Others' involved	Preparation	Actions
08.00– 11.00	Check US and client emails with day plan	30 minutes	PA for part	Plan from previous day	PA actions
	Briefing of new holiday cover plan	90 minutes	Section leaders (SLs)	Check with HR on core parts of briefing	SLs able to brief their teams
				Develop slides	
11.00– 13.00	Understand updated policy on new accounts	50 minutes	Manager and other section leaders	Check current policy. Read advance documentation	Put together briefing sheet for teams
	Progress against plan check	15 minutes	PA		PA respond to calls/ emails
	Lunch	20 minutes	HR manager	Catch up	
13.00– 15.00	Agreed individual performance plans	45 minutes × 2	Two of section leaders	Read notes written on day 1	Both parties take away and check before signing off

15.00–18.00 18.30	Draft copy of exec. report and presentation	90 minutes		Copy of previous report plus initial notes	Send to AA for checking
	Check day figures	15 minutes		Information from SLs	Check out any issues?
	Plan for day 3	20 minutes		PA	Diary for day 3 online
	Tennis lesson	90 minutes			

Notice that there are spaces built in for other activities that emerge, preparation slots and time for reflection/decision making. She now felt better prepared, was more confident in presenting her ideas, stuck to meeting times and set a more positive time management example for her reports and colleagues.

2 Set aside periods of time to do specific types of activity

A lot of people find that they are much more productive when they chunk work into blocks of time that require similar approaches or skills. This can include having times during the day when you only read and respond to essential emails, or make calls. This creates the additional bonus of allowing you to stay focussed on one thing at a time rather than constantly having to adjust your concentration. Another element that many people find invaluable is to structure a time early in the morning to plan and deal with tasks from previous days. This freeing-up process can make it much easier to focus on and deal with additional tasks, as they arise. Again, at the end of the day it can be useful to have a slot to acknowledge what has been completed and decide what needs to be parked, deferred or quickly acted upon. In this way, a stronger sense of purpose is achieved and less baggage is taken home with you.

3 Educate others to know when you will be available

It is reasonable for you to set out and let others know the specific times of the day when you are available to deal with their enquiries and respond to the demands they may have. By offering alternative timings to meet or discuss important activities, you will be supporting your and others' planning. If you do not do these things you will find yourself operating from an entirely reactive position, where it feels as if others have control over when you do things.

Personal case study

A group I worked with also used an educating process to indicate to others the state of availability they were in at any time of day. Little flags or signs were visible as people approached and showed whether they were free to talk [green], open to talk if it was urgent or important [orange] and 'in no way should they be approached or spoken to', unless a disaster was taking place [red].

This may seem trite but it worked for them, and avoided many unnecessary interruptions and reduced any potential dilemmas and confrontations.

4 Be specific and clear about time agreements

Whenever you are asking others to undertake work for you, always ensure that your expectations are communicated in ways that show you are being realistic about what is achievable. By scoping your work clearly, others will understand what you need and are less likely to produce something that requires you or them to take extra, correcting time. Using emails, it is always helpful to be as specific as possible about the type of response and when you need it. I receive so many emails that are vague and ambiguous about what I am expected to do. Get in the habit of giving instructions that make life easier for others and, ultimately, yourself.

5 You will be interrupted, so make best choices about whether you need to deal with a request or a demand at that particular point

It is wise to accept that interruptions happen and you will have to deal with them in ways that help you and others to make the best decisions about what needs to be done. The first step is to identify how important and urgent any activity is that you are being asked to take on.

I have devised a set of questions that can help you to identify who can best do the work, when and how, by attaching a more objective level of need to the activity. They work particularly well when I am unsure about the importance of any demand and am left querying the reasonableness of demand or timescales.

Activity

Prioritising the work requested by others

Think of a task you recently accepted from someone else, that may have left you feeling irritated or it seemed to be a much lower priority to you than to them. Complete these questions based on that task.

What do my strong work values tell me about this activity?

What am I here to do and does this activity fit within this description?

How does this activity fit with the bigger picture of what we are trying to achieve as a function or project group?

To what extent does this activity motivate, challenge, stimulate and satisfy my needs?

How important is this activity [1 = Critical to the business, 5 = Nice to do at some point]?

What will be affected if I take this activity on now?

Why is it a priority for others?

How realistic are the proposed timescales?

What does this now tell you about the task, and other similar activities that you may undertake?

6 Beware the number of 'monkeys' you are collecting

Learn to push back more, encourage others to answer their own questions and delegate tasks to them.

I have come across many examples that illustrate the principle that staff are more adept at delegating to their bosses, rather than the other way around. You may be able to associate with this. 'Monkeys' are tasks that other people expect us to take on when they ask, even if we are not the best person to deal with them. For many people, however, facing demands and pressures from different directions, it can appear a constant battle to resist what these other people, who are usually part of our key relationships network, are asking them to take on.

Personal case study

Elaine, a middle manager, described her morning to me during our first coaching session. She had walked through the door and immediately faced a colleague asking for help with a client issue. As she approached her desk, the phone rang and her boss stated he needed the report she was working on within the hour. She noted that one of her staff was ill, so she had to drop everything and reallocate activities within her team, including deciding to do some of the activities herself. Finally, when she got to read her emails, she discovered a set of questions, marked URGENT, that had come in from a supplier overnight. It was 09.30 am and four 'monkeys' already had taken up residence on her shoulders and she had not begun work on anything in her original plan! Once in place, these monkeys can also require constant feeding.

Like Elaine, are you collecting monkeys throughout the day? If so, consider, as she did, when you need to have conversations with your protagonists about what is possible and important to you achieving what you are there to do. It is also about deciding what will produce the best outcomes for the business.

7 Put time into what you can change and influence, not what you can't

Many people put enormous amounts of time and energy into attempting to change the elements of their work and life which they have very little control or influence over. As you proceed down this course it is easier to become disappointed, feel powerless and experience 'failure'. If this is a tendency for you, then soon it will evolve into a negative pattern.

Personal case study

I joined a large financial organisation and, for the first three months, it felt like I was operating in an alien land. As an idealist and self-appointed 'change agent',

I wanted to bring about changes that I believed would make a significant shift in the way we operated. This only began to change when I realised that I was getting involved in too many tasks where I had not yet built up my credibility and influence or established trusting relationships. I was not at the point where others would be prepared to listen to me. They also rightly questioned my input, given my short period of financial services experience and lack of cultural understanding.

Are you one of those people who run into stone walls, take on issues of global business significance or engage in attempts to change your whole organisation?

Locus of control and influence

I have developed a useful maxim that goes 'Get your own role clear and under control first, then, build your influence to affect other people and bigger areas.'

Activity

Take a moment to step back and use the diagram overleaf, to help you think of relevant examples of your influence and control.

Where do you actually have control over what happens to you and others?

Where can you influence others to bring about change, and do what you think is needed?

What is interesting for you personally, but may be outside of your control and influence right now?

Where do you have no control or influence over the situation, people, strategy or policies?

Where do you need to stop tilting at windmills and focus on areas you can do something about, that will help to bring about the changes that you believe will reduce pressure on you and others?

Take time to identify where you want the activities that you are currently undertaking to fit in the future.

What is within the focus of my control and influence?

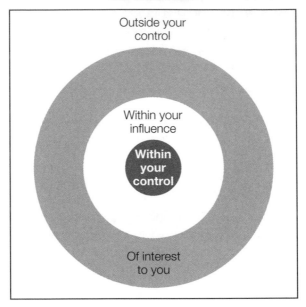

Source: Adapted from Stephen Covey, *The Seven Habits of Highly Effective People*, Schuster 1994.

8 Be realistic about how long activities will take

When you operate in a fast-moving, crowded environment, it is easy to believe that you can take on anything, and complete everything quickly. This usually pushes you and others to overload your diary and underestimate realistic target points. We also try to impress people by demonstrating what we can do above the norm. It's a way of enabling us to stand out from the crowd, or so we think!

Here are a few ways you can prevent developing the 'over-promise/under-deliver (OPUD) syndrome':

→ Add 10 per cent extra time to each task and project up front. This will give you some leeway and flexibility to allow for disruptions, changes and additional demands.

→ Get inputs from others involved who are familiar with the areas you are addressing.

- → Always negotiate what is possible and how long it will take. Do not just accept what others tell you about timelines and delivery points.
- → Keep others informed of changes and provide opportunities to review progress and renegotiate completion dates.
- → Do not schedule any meetings back-to-back, which will allow for some over-run.

9 Allow regular breaks to recharge your batteries and restore your focus and sharpen your concentration

I've described to you examples of days where there is little or no relief from endless activity, meetings, briefings, presentations, interviews, reviews ...

Do you rush out of the house in the morning (without breakfast), conduct back-to-back sessions throughout the day, snatch a sandwich at your desk (if you are lucky), and work on something for hours at a time, often using mesmerising technology? It has been shown that people who do these things experience more losses in concentration, major energy dips and make a greater number of mistakes in their work. Is this continuously frenzied activity really any good for your personal or professional health?

Personal case study

I recently worked with an office manager, Mark, who had realised that his people fitted this action-oriented pattern. After our discussion and consulting with his team, he agreed that he and the team would:

- → take a break from their technology every hour;
- → move about or do something physical throughout the day (a good chance to actually talk with colleagues);
- → at points where energy levels were low, eat healthy snacks (that he provided or made available);
- → drink copious amounts of water, and fewer carbonated drinks;
- → speak with as many people as possible in the office at least once a day, face-to-face, about how things were going and check who needed support;
- → whenever it was possible, take lunch together, away from their desks.

What do these ideas suggest to you that you could do to sometimes slow the pace of the day, and encourage others to take breaks that will boost everyone's energy?

10 Develop good habits for leaving work, travelling and spending time away from home

Something that many people have become poor at is the ability to close down our work day and make the adjustments needed to move into our personal and social lives with energy and ease. The effect of this is less time spent with loved ones, fewer social engagements, and reduced sporting or cultural activity time. The biggest impact, however, comes about when you realise how little time and energy you are spending on yourself. It is you who gets short-changed the most!

Personal case study

During my work with an engineering group, as part of their assessment of how well they did with taking care of themselves and others, they identified this over-working pattern as a typical issue. They came up with some creative ideas for winning back time to be with others who mattered most, and gave a greater chance of doing more of the things that really mattered for themselves. Here are some of their 'freedom rules':

→ Do not start pieces of work after 5 pm because what we start we usually stay with until we finish.
→ Develop a plan for next actions before 5 pm, where there is unfinished business.
→ Make bookings for events involving others, on at least two nights of the week.
→ Allocate one evening a week as 'just for me time'.
→ No meetings to extend beyond 5.30 pm.
→ Dedicate an email-only time, mid-afternoon, allowing time specifically to respond only to those that are considered important.
→ There will be a team member award each month for the person who achieves most in this process.
→ On Fridays, we do something together in the early evening, which means we all shut down.

Consider the experience of this group and apply it to your own situation.

Which of these ideas will you adopt?

Who else will you need to involve in this process?

What additional ideas does it trigger for you?

What is the one thing you will change immediately?

That leaves one important area that will help you to win back control of at least some of your time, and do the right things. This is the ability to **negotiate what is possible, achievable and reasonable**. There are probably times when you have accepted the tasks that others have demanded or asked of you and were left feeling concerned about whether you should be doing them, or frustrated that you took them on. It is essential that at the point of acceptance or agreement discussions take place about the validity of the activity, its priority and how it fits within your overall workload.

With my clients I develop a set of best practice responses based on their understanding of the people and the organisation. At the heart of these practices are four elements:

1   How important is the activity or task? If you refer back to the structure I recommended earlier in the chapter, you will be able to carry out your analysis to help decide the level of priority and importance.

2   Find appropriate ways of saying 'no', when you have a strong case for not taking on an additional or new activity. It is more influential to state your case briefly, strongly, and with valid reasons that will be meaningful to the other person. You could say, 'I am not able to take on that task right now as I need to commit all of the next two days to this report for the exec,' or 'I can't do it, as I don't have access to that information.'

3   You or the other person provide an alternative option. This is not saying a blanket 'no', it is exploring alternatives, such as, 'I can't be involved in this, but David in Finance is experienced in dealing with that. I suggest you approach him,' or 'This won't be possible for me right now but I can get some of my team to work on it next week.'

4 If it still feels like you are being put under pressure to do the work, it pays to state the consequences of you doing that activity. Bosses and other senior people are sometimes unaware of your other commitments and they can make the final call only if they know what the affect will be. Tell them, 'If I take that on this week, the presentation for the director will not get done. Do you want me to do that or will you find someone else to prepare the presentation?'

There are times when you will not get an immediate acceptance of what you are asking for. In these cases you may need to restate your position or put it back to the other person to help you find a way of resolving your dilemma.

So, the five options available to you in any situation are:

→ Consider and plan how and when you want to say no.

→ Negotiate based on alternatives.

→ Find another option that will appeal to others.

→ State the effect and consequences of you accepting the task.

→ Hold your ground and restate your position when necessary.

Consider a recent piece of work that you took on that put you under pressure. Identify what sort of conversation you would have now and what you would say that would influence the other person.

If you do not have these conversations on a regular basis you are likely to become even more overloaded and your pressure levels will rise.

Summary

This chapter has asked you to consider where you are not using your time as productively as you might. You have then worked on a number of pressure areas, so that you can develop some fresh thinking about how you can improve your time usage. Finally, you will have considered how you can have conversations with others to reduce the excessive demands you face and operate on the basis of what is truly achievable and realistic.

The four key points for doing less with sufficient time are:

→ Plan every week and include aspects of your life outside work.
→ Always understand the real priority and importance of tasks before you accept them.
→ Involve others in your planning and in activities that will raise energy and generate action.
→ Know when it's time to stop and move on.

Until you value yourself, you won't value your time. Until you value your time, you will not do anything with it. M. SCOTT PECK

Developing coping tactics that work

Chapter Three

The problem is never the problem – the coping is the problem. VIRGINIA SATIR

In the short term, we all develop our own preferred ways of conserving or recharging our energy throughout a working day and week. These are often referred to as coping tactics, as they help us to slow the effects of pressure or deal with it in ways that mean we reach the end of the day or the weekend in a reasonably healthy state. One of your tasks, if you are to be successful in surviving tough days and weeks, is to consider what you are currently using as coping tactics and check whether they are helping you to, at least, hold your own.

From my clients' experience, these are some of the more common coping tactics that a lot of people use. Use this as a checklist to identify which ones you draw upon regularly to keep yourself going and top up your energy.

→ Express your feelings strongly, cry, shout, rant.
→ Talk to friends/family, colleagues, boss, staff, your team.
→ Engage in vigorous exercise, e.g. run, gym work, swim, walk, zumba.
→ Take stimulants, e.g. coffee, alcohol, cigarettes, Red Bull.
→ Take yourself off to a quiet place to get your thinking straight.
→ Make a decision.
→ Set new goals.
→ Put energy and effort into working with/helping others.
→ Take prescribed drugs, medication.
→ Listen to or play music, sing, dance.
→ Practise yoga, meditation, Pilates.
→ Use a sauna, steam room, massage.
→ Work harder, longer hours.
→ Eat chocolate, crisps, biscuits, cakes, puddings.
→ Spend money, e.g. retail therapy.
→ Party/socialise.

→ Positively challenge what is happening.

→ Watch films/TV/play online games.

→ Play with your children and/or animals.

→ Sit and do nothing.

→ Sleep for longer or at different times.

→ Therapy, counselling, phone support lines.

→ Complementary health support, e.g. acupuncture, osteopathy, homeopathy.

→ Laugh out loud.

→ Discuss issues with a coach or mentor.

The first thing you will probably notice is how few of these tactics you regularly make use of. Now take time to think which you could use more regularly to preserve your health state or enable you to be in a better position to deal with difficulties or concerns.

It is also important to consider which tactics you are using that may not help with the situations you are facing and the pressures you are experiencing. In fact, some of these actions often will give you only a short fix, suppress the pain or lessen your fears for a short time. They may not address the cause of the pressure and may even leave you in a worse state. My favourite example is red wine. One glass at the end of a tough day or when I need my spirits raising, generally works well. Three or four glasses will leave me experiencing disturbed sleep, hangover symptoms, difficulty concentrating and tiredness the next day.

What is it that you do, that may be having an unhelpful effect?

Is your prop coffee, retail therapy, taking your problems out on someone else, or relying on prescribed drugs?

Where you have identified tactics that do not deal with the pressure you face, consider how you might regularly adopt and use the ideas in my top 10 list that follows. This is particularly relevant for times when you are facing a number of challenges and experiencing important changes.

My top 10 tactics based on observations of what produces the most lasting results

1 **Express your feelings strongly, at the time when pressure occurs.** Throughout the day, as you experience a series of demands and have difficult encounters, you may contain your feelings and not do anything to counter the effect of the adrenaline and other hyperactive chemicals that course through your body. To counter the effects of these stress-related changes, including raised blood pressure, you need to have a release mechanism. Different things work for different people, but putting yourself in situations where you can have a good shout, cry, laugh outrageously, hit out at an inanimate object, or even scream, can provide some release. A milder, and perhaps wiser, alternative in the workplace will be for you to find the most appropriate person and express to them the effect they and the situation are having on you. We will explore this further, in Chapter Five, when you consider managing your relationships in different ways in order to reduce pressure.

2 **Take vigorous exercise to provide a rapid release state and a rebalancing of energy.** We often experience the need to vent anger, discharge frustration and combat boredom. Activity will help you to rebalance the chemical elements in your body, ultimately enabling you to focus, be calm and respond rationally. Is there an activity that gets you back on track and, when you take part in it, you know it boosts your energy and improves your mood? Can you consider running, swimming, fast walking, dancing, Zumba, playing squash or football?

3 **Use therapeutic help** to provide a sounding board, and a safe place where you are listened to without being judged or told what to do. Employee Assistance Programmes provide an important way that organisations can support their staff. They offer neutral, yet empathetic, counselling and advisory support and are the first place I would encourage you to go if you are anxious about your state of mind, unsatisfactory relationships, financial or legal affairs. It is a courageous step to make the call or arrange to see a counsellor, yet we know the difference it can make to have a safe environment and confidential process within which to discuss

personal challenges and issues. It will be better for you and others to make a call earlier, than allowing the situation to develop and leave you in a high pressure state.

4 **Relax** in a slowing activity or practice. This is provided most easily through activities like Pilates, yoga, meditation, body work and deep massage. They particularly induce energy release when it appears that your energy has locked up or you feel stuck. Physical treatments of many types are readily available in some enlightened organisations. These employers and managers recognise the big changes that can build up in the positive emotional, physical and mental state of their people. Most simply at your desk or workstation you can gently exercise or meditate at points throughout the day, without others being particularly aware or concerned about what you are doing. It will make an enormous difference to your energy, concentration and, ultimately, productivity. Many Asian businesses have, for a long time, encouraged their workforce to be involved in activity such as tai chi, when low energy points are likely to occur that they know will affect problem solving, decision making and focus.

5 **Tuning out, or in,** to music, radio and television or electronic games can involve immersing yourself in a sensory environment that allows people to switch off strong emotions, and let them go. Focussed relaxation also displaces negative thoughts that are generating tension. Playing certain types of music has been shown to be very beneficial in helping with emotional control for hyperactive children, patients or creating a calmer state in institutions such as prisons. If it works in harsh environments like these, then what difference will it make in your average office, depot or plant?

6 **Partying and socialising** provide a means of release when you need to let your hair down, blow out pent-up energy or immerse in social behaviour that takes you outside of yourself or allows you to positively engage with others. Positive social engagement also recreates the feelings we have experienced at times when we were able to loosen the controls and restraints that we associate with tension. We feel valued, appreciated and liked as ourselves.

7 **Playing with animals or children** has always been something that, for many of us, provides a sense of grounding and it was a

necessary reality check for me, particularly when I arrived home after having a testing day. They do not ask you to do anything but focus your positive attention on them and immerse yourself in meeting their needs. In the process you will get unconditional love, attention and sensory contact, which often is missing during the rest of the day.

8 **Sleeping** will enable your body to recover, shut down and take you out of the conscious pressure state, allowing you to relax to the REM sleep point where your unconscious takes over. On many occasions I have woken from a good sleep, knowing exactly what I need to do, or with an issue now seeming much more manageable. What difference does a good sleep make for you? Can you take power naps, a siesta or short shut-downs? In many cultures this is the norm.

9 **Phoning or texting a friend** has become the first port of call and favourite form of discharge for many of us. When we are confused, don't know what to do or face a decision that is leaving us in an anxious state, contacting someone you trust usually works. We trust them to know how to best support and appropriately challenge us. They often provide the means or the obvious route to our moving on. However, many of us, at times, do not trust others enough to support us, or we find it difficult to ask for help. Who will you contact first when you are stuck?

10 **Taking yourself off** to a place where you can have quiet, space and an environment that feels calming has become critical for people who work consistently in a noisy, open-plan situation or in close contact with many others throughout the day. In these environments there is little let-up, particularly for those who enjoy their own company and who, in order to concentrate, prefer to be free from interruption. For many, these conditions prove difficult and draining. Where is your haven of quiet? Where can you go to enjoy a moment's peace? Where is your best thinking and planning space?

Now, take a few minutes to note ways that you could more often recharge your batteries.

There is, not surprisingly, a level with many of these support mechanisms where we can have too much of a good thing. Do you know what your tipping point is? When do you go too far and what is the effect?

Personal case study

Sam described herself as a therapy junkie. When she experienced a rise in tension, she sought the help of a squadron of health practitioners. The result was often confusing assessment and diagnosis, and the prescription of a collection of remedies, exercises and treatments that appeared to work to restore her health balance. Following our work, she agreed that the most powerful restorative solutions came about when she confided in and talked with close family and friends. She also acknowledged that there were work colleagues whom she trusted but did not use when she was under pressure. She felt at her best when she took the time to cook wholesome food such as soups and stews.

We often find that the simple, accessible and low-cost solutions are often the best. Are there safety valves that you take for granted or don't consider making use of?

How do you keep yourself going at work?

Whilst we often have a range of strategies for supporting ourselves outside of work, many of us do not take the same care to develop coping mechanisms within our workplaces. Given a day involving a procession of challenging activities, back-to-back meetings and time constraints to complete work, the need for escape routes and recharging is even more important. So how can you build your energy and sustain it? I want to focus on the areas that people discuss with us most frequently. All my research shows that it is in these areas that you can make the biggest differences and, if you are not using them to make progress and perhaps save your day, then it's time to start.

→ **Talk with someone who can help, e.g. your boss, colleagues, staff** It is okay to get input from others who are in a position to help you, particularly when you feel stuck or uncertain about which direction to take. Often we just need a nudge or words of encouragement to take that next step.

→ **Take time out or move away from your normal workstation** Being away from the problem or in a different environment can provide a very different perspective. Using a quiet room, space outside or café area can all provide a catalyst for thinking differently.

→ **Have a complete break** After a prolonged period of concentration and focussed activity, doing something completely different 'refreshes the parts'. Deliberately planning or taking a chunk of time to engage in something very different can feel restful and aide recuperation, after a tiring period.

→ **Put energy into others** When we get caught up in our own concerns, it is sometimes helpful to invest energy in supporting others to help them achieve or learn something. Focussing on what others need can take us away from our anxious selves.

→ **Do nothing** There are times when it is better to sit still, contemplate, reflect and allow things to happen without our interference, rather than moving in an unhelpful direction or working harder at the same thing.

→ **Alternatively, do something active** Moving and doing something physical, even going up and down steps, will provide a new charge or allow you to deal with the soporific effects of sitting at your desk or being physically inactive. This is an essential discipline for those who are bound to a static workstation for long periods. If you feel lethargic, shake anything that will move. This deskercise could become the new fad.

→ **Make a decision and get into action** When we are going in circles or procrastinating, any decision is often better than none and is a step forward. The worst direction you can take normally is to seek more information or carry out further analysis. If in doubt, do something and watch carefully for the response or result you get. You can always do something else if your initial plan doesn't work out. Doing nothing for a great length of time often achieves nothing.

→ **Deal with the problem** By challenging what or who is creating an issue, you are more likely to influence what happens, and tackling the source of work pressure is a great place to start. Too often, we end up taking out our frustrations on some unsuspecting victim, who merely generates the last straw.

Activity

Now take time to consider how you cope at work currently and what you can add to your repertoire.

What works for you?

What do others around you do successfully, that you could include in your coping tactics?

Which of these suggestions is something you want and intend to do more of?

How can you have energy throughout your day sufficient to deal with pressure?

There are three areas of your life that can dramatically influence the amount of sustainable energy you have, and enable you to feel strong enough to deal successfully with pressure situations. Maintaining your daily energy reservoir is dependent largely on you getting sufficient high-quality sleep, reasonable physical activity and building an appropriate eating regime.

The three core ingredients in building your energy reservoir

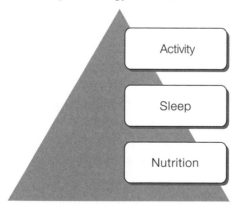

Activity

Sleep

Nutrition

Eating to have sufficient energy

Having the energy you need throughout your day will critically affect your ability to deal with pressures and difficult, changing situations.

Does your daily energy pattern look like a constantly changing line graph involving peaks and troughs? If so, then you need to consider your eating habits, timings, balance and amounts of food that is forcing your energy system to spike and then plummet.

To what extent does your breakfast set you up for a positive start to the day, and experience energy levels that last for most of the morning?

Are the snacks you eat throughout the day full of sugars? If so consider the dramatic rise in type 2 diabetes and stop now! Keep a supply of fruit and nuts handy.

Are you having small amounts of balanced food, regularly throughout the day? If so you will maintain higher energy levels, for longer.

Are you keeping yourself going with caffeine drinks? The more you do this the more you will need to consume, creating a constant spiral of highs and lows that put excessive pressure on your vital organs. Go for water, juice, and alternative teas.

Are you having heavy, large meals in the evening to make up for not eating throughout the day? Consider the effect this is having on your digestive system, and how your sleep may be affected!

A typically imbalanced daily eating and energy pattern

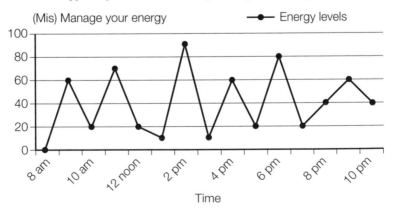

Source: Jeff Archer, www.the-tonic.com

Consider the eating and energy mismanagement model and ask yourself, does your eating pattern lead you to go through days where you experience constant highs and lows, created by sugar-loaded food and snacks which force your pancreas to produce excess insulin?

How can you counter this pattern with a better daily nutritional regime?

What would you include in your new regime and when would you eat differently?

Consider the following food energy habits

Start your day with a smaller energy boost that is sustainable. Many people have got into the habit of starting their day with coffee, buns and fatty foods, wondering why they have an energy dip later in the morning. At that point, those easily accessible chocolate bars and biscuits merely produce another sugar spike followed by a bigger dip. I suggest you go with porridge, good cereals, granary bread, fruit, eggs, live yoghurt and fish.

Throughout your day consider your overall balance of proteins, carbohydrates and fruit and vegetables. If your typical lunch is high on pasta or bread, leave them out along with the piles of potatoes and rice, during the rest of the day.

As you need snacks or top-ups, get used to eating fresh fruit, decent cereal bars, nuts, dried fruit, vegetable crisps, crudités, natural yoghurt and fruit smoothies. There is so much choice available and you do not have to buy all the processed food that is full of sugar and salt. You and your family do not need them and they will soon eat what they get used to.

Cook from fresh. If you do not have much time, buy one of those excellent cookbooks for easy, quick meals. Most processed and ready meals will have high salt or sugar content, as do many low-fat foods. You think you are eating well because they taste good, but it's time for all of us to learn more about what we eat and discover those hidden sugars. It is these hidden sugars that contribute most to energy spikes and dips throughout the day, as well as producing extra fat build-up.

Eating smaller amounts more often is a better regime than one very large meal at night. The size of portion that meets our requirements for main meals is the equivalent of two handfuls, not four or five 'pile highs'. We get hungry for these amounts because we do not eat well, we have built up large portion habits and we do not spread our balanced intake throughout the day.

So, if you want to have more energy and maintain a reasonable level of healthy energy, without the common highs and lows, then it is totally up to you to change the amount, frequency, quality and type of food you eat. You won't need any diet if this is combined with sufficient physical activity. It is usually easier if others around you are willing to eat in the same way.

How do I get a good sleep and wake up feeling refreshed?

The key to this is evident when we notice and copy what children do. They sleep best when they have a routine pattern and are undisturbed by anxious thoughts or environmental disturbance. Think about a time when you had a wonderful night of relaxed sleep and woke refreshed and keen to make the most of your day. What was it that made the difference for you?

Here are some ways that I have identified for you to set up a way of sleeping that will make a difference, particularly to the amount of energy you start your day with.

Sleep for approximately the same time, each night, including weekends. This is unlike many people I encounter who stay up late, get up early and then bank their sleep into the weekends. Also consider what your ideal sleep time period is. Margaret Thatcher was a rarity, needing only four hours. Most of us need an average of eight hours and there is strong support for getting as much head-down as possible, before midnight.

Linked to this, each of us has our favourite means of relaxation, and these are ideal for getting us in the mood to go to bed and sleep well. Common examples include warm baths, reading, listening to music, hot drinks and meditation or yoga. Educate your brain to attach 'sleep thinking', when you do something relaxing during the evening. This does not mean chilling out as a couch potato in front of the television and waking up at 2 am, in a dishevelled state.

Too many people use a range of technology close to their sleep time, and this generally agitates or stimulates our thinking, so that we are switched on when we close our eyes. As a regular practice, stop laptop, mobile or iPad time at least an hour before going to bed.

Eating big, heavy meals late in the evening will mean that your digestive system is fully at work throughout much of the night, often disturbing your sleep pattern. It can also leave you feeling uncomfortable and heavy in bed.

Wherever possible, make your bedroom a haven for sleep. Use decoration and colours that you like and that calm you. Put in softer lighting, install decent blackout curtains, get rid of clutter and buy a comfortable mattress and pillows. The way you set up your bedroom needs to convey pleasure, relaxation and restfulness.

Avoid using stimulants throughout your evening, such as coffee, tea, Red Bull, tobacco and drugs. There are herbs like verbena, chamomile and lavender that can encourage sleepiness. Many clients swear by warm milk drinks to finally set them off.

Take time to close off from the busy activity of the day. You are likely to achieve this by following a pattern of close down that you know enables you to feel secure.

Deal with any unfinished business. It's almost impossible to switch off if there are calls not made, arguments in midstream, critical actions not taken and decisions pending. It's particularly difficult to move from one incomplete activity to another without an element of closure. If there are anxieties hanging in the air, find your best person to talk with or at least provide an opportunity to get your emotional energy out. I find that writing down lingering thoughts at some point during the evening, then capturing what I will do with them the next day and finally putting the book away, helps me to close out the day.

Finally, look at spending a little on the new light-based technology for providing a less-stressed form of wake-up call.

Considering the above recommendations, how could you increase the chances of your sleeping well this evening? What will get you to leap out of bed tomorrow and want to be at work?

If in doubt, have a bath, give and receive a massage, enjoy sex or read a really good book.

Using physical activity that works for you to boost energy

My approach is very simple and will make a difference to your energy and overall health state by following these six guidelines:

1 Do something that you will enjoy, and that meets your and others' needs. Activities like dance, Zumba, spinning, water aerobics and Pilates provide a social contact point for many people and will enable you to feel part of a group. Hopefully you are also having fun whilst the calories come off.

2 Consider activity as also being about building your strength, dexterity and suppleness, which, as we get older, becomes a stronger need for most people. If you build or repair things, work in the garden, or maintain a house, you will have a physical activity that also focusses on achieving and producing something that is aesthetically and practically pleasing.

3 Get involved in activities that require a commitment and generate a sense of support for others. The team element of many activities promotes the values of support, loyalty, commitment and determination that are at the heart of resilience. You are most likely to be disciplined about committing to action if you have agreed with others to be part of something. It is more likely that you will get out of work and to a venue in the evening when you have committed to others and know you will not let them down. Consider the success of rambling clubs, flash events, singing groups and the growth of dance classes.

4 Whatever you do, do it regularly if you want to make progress or build fitness. Fifteen minutes of high intensity activity each day is better than occasional involvement in the odd longer bout of exercise. Getting into a routine can encourage you to keep going and want to achieve more or improve.

5 Those who sustain an activity usually set themselves goals that provide a driver and reinforcement to continue to make progress. These can be observed, felt and measured. Notice the drive of someone committed to completing a run, ride or swim, in order to raise money for a charity. Our own pride in success can also provide a powerful prompt. I meet a lot of clients who want to look good for an occasion, fit into nice clothes for a holiday, or complete a

distance or time they have not achieved before. Even if it's climbing stairs without puffing, sleeping without wheezing or reaching a pub at the end of a walk, having desirable outcomes is likely to prompt a stronger sense of discipline in you to sustain your efforts and to make a difference.

6 Celebrating success has become a lost art in many organisations and is often missing in our 'take it for granted' personal lives. We assume that hard work and putting effort into something is just the norm. My completion of the London Marathon, in a really slow time, finishing with the elephants, rhinos and other creatures, was one of my proudest moments. And I celebrated for weeks, including as many people as possible who had supported me.

But it does not have to be a major event. Celebrating as you hit progress markers along the way is a powerful reinforcement to continue an important recognition of your efforts so far.

Activity

Ask yourself these questions:

What are you now prompted to get out there and take part in?

What will this activity enable you to achieve or do?

What will success be like?

How will you celebrate?

Many people on their recovery path, after experiencing chronic stress situations, have stated that the biggest contributing factor was to ensure that they took part in activities that provided the energy they needed to deal with things that previously might have beaten them.

Give yourself a break

In your busy world, how can you get some breathing space?

Given the pace and intensity of most jobs, what we really need is to find regular breathing space to give us time to deal effectively with the immediate demands that are coming from all directions. A simple yet powerful key is to be able to adjust your breathing in the immediately pressured situation. When we experience difficulties, we tend to take short, quick and shallow breaths. This gives a warning signal to our brain that all is not well and we move into a fight or flight response. This is a pattern that can happen frequently throughout the typical work day. With our body on high alert, we put strain on our coping resources and constant burden on our vital organs. No wonder we experience chest pains, tightening sensations, muscular aches, run out of breath and feel anxious.

Learn first to keep breathing

By slowing down what we do whilst taking strong breaths, with deliberate pauses, we signal to our nervous system that we are in control and can manage.

Here is a little exercise you can do anywhere, if you are experiencing concerns about a situation you are anxious about.

Activity

Get yourself in a comfortable position and notice how you are breathing.

Put your hand on your abdomen and allow your lungs to slowly fill.

When your abdomen and lungs feel fully expanded, breath out slowly through your mouth, and then **PAUSE** for three seconds.

Repeat this process four times.

Now notice your controlled breathing and how differently you feel.

Breathing like this means that you get more oxygen to your brain and vital organs, which in turn provides the energy you need to think about and respond to situations with clarity and purpose.

As a coping habit, do this exercise at least twice a day, when it's all getting too much. And remember, if you are about to start an important meeting, discussion, interview or presentation, breathing with pause could be your trump card for success and confidence.

Knowing when to stop

There is a stage in most tasks when you will get to the point of diminishing returns. It is easy then to continue through the tiredness and low-energy barrier, increasing the likelihood of making mistakes, jumbling our thoughts and producing poorer quality work. You will feel and experience these points and begin to know when it is best to consider taking a break, doing something different or moving completely away from the task or your workstation.

Something you can do quickly involves making an intentional shift for a short space of time by switching from doing and activity to being and awareness. Use the following table as a guide.

Doing and activity	*Being and awareness*
Planning	Observing what is there
Organising	Your thoughts
Creating	Your feelings
Strategising	Your bodily sensations
Remembering	The environment
Communicating	Your breathing
Reflecting	
Evaluating	

Moving from doing to being as a strategy when you are under pressure

For a short time, instead of putting pressure on yourself to make decisions, judgements and take actions, purely observe what is there, accept everything that is happening is valid and remove any pressure on yourself to have to 'get it right'. Write down what you have observed and noticed. You may find it enlightening and creative as you notice a rise in the quality of your work and differences in the way you engage with others in their work activity.

As a starting point decide on a small activity that often appears to drain your energy or leaves you weary. For today, replace it with five minutes of being, by focussing on what is there and, at the end, record what you were aware of.

Four examples of times where you can use deliberate pause and conscious awareness are:

→ Catching yourself reading an email or paragraph of a report for the third time. What is going on for you at this point? What can you focus on that will shift you in your activity?

→ Noticing when you are concerned about what you will say in a meeting. Listen to the thoughts without judging. Notice your reaction to the different thoughts.

→ Writing 'keep breathing' and 'pause' on a document going into a high-paced communication situation and making it easily observed throughout the exchange.

→ Using a calm interrupting sound set on your alarm, computer or watch that will interrupt you during a long task and remind you gently to take a break or switch off.

Summary

In this chapter you have explored a diverse range of tactics that will help you to build your energy and maintain it. This will ensure that you have the best internal coping mechanisms available when you start to come under pressure.

As a starter, identify coping tactics that you can add to your repertoire and check to see that they will help you to deal with the issues that are generating pressure for you. Are you using tactics that leave you feeling in a worse position or those that have helped you to deal with situations and move forward?

Both inside and outside of work, are you making best use of the opportunities, resources, people and energisers that will ensure that you get through the week in a reasonably sane, satisfied and healthy state?

If you know that you have energy fluctuations throughout your days, it is likely that some element of your sleep, activity and nutrition habits have a part to play in this. Consider the options raised and make a choice to change one element in each of these areas, starting **now**!

When you find yourself in a period of high-paced, continuous, demanding work, identify times when you will take time out, pause and notice what is happening. Each of these practices will take only a short time but will pay enormous dividends in helping you to remain focussed, remember what you need to and continue with energy to produce high-quality work.

If it's getting too much, **pause, breathe, observe, slow down**.

Tactics mean doing what you can with what you have. SAUL ALINSKY

Thinking positively when it feels difficult

Chapter Four

> **Pressure is a word that is misused in our vocabulary. When you start thinking of pressure, it's because you've started to think of failure.** TOMMY LASORDA

One of the fundamental aspects of our ability to deal with pressure situations is the absolute relationship between our perception of what is happening, what we then think, the feelings that follow and, ultimately, our response to situations. Once we accept this to be true then we feel empowered to make changes when we are under pressure, based on knowing that we have a range of choices. We also do not have to accept the first or most obvious option that becomes available. This pattern of response is often based on what we have learnt to do, rather than us actively and consciously dealing with what we are facing. In the following figure, you can see how each of these elements is connected and activated, as a key part of our way of responding to difficulties.

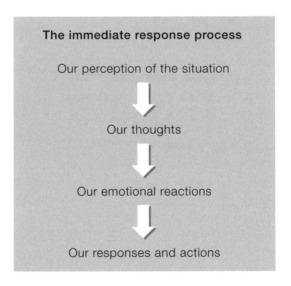

Imagine this common scenario ... you are driving on a motorway when suddenly a car passes you at great speed, then pulls in front of you and breaks quickly! In the short period this has been happening, your brain and the rest of your body systems have been put on high alert. This could be your saving grace or your downfall, depending on the sequence you choose to run through. If you follow a typically negative response process, this is what may occur ...

The **perception** of the situation that you go with is that you are aware that the other driver has taken some actions that have created a situation that is highly dangerous and has put you at risk.

As a result, you are **thinking** 'What an idiot' (this is the polite version).

The **feelings** you experience are, 'I feel angry (and probably afraid).'

As a result of the above elements, your **response** is to close the gap, shout abuse, and flash your lights. These are actions that could escalate into conflict and increase the risk to yourself and others.

An **alternative positive process** makes use of all the skills and knowledge you have available in this scenario and would follow this sequence.

Your **perception** is that there is potentially a danger, you are alert to the options and are conscious of ways of removing yourself safely from the situation. You say, 'What do I need to do to be safe?'

Your **thinking** is clear and focussed, and you are saying to yourself, 'I need to be extra careful' and 'I have to concentrate on what I do and watch out for further changes, for myself and others to be okay.'

You **feel** calmer, steadier and confident about your driving skills and awareness of possibilities.

In **response**, you slow up, ease back or pull in at a service area for a hot drink.

What this clearly illustrates is the effect that our thinking has on the ways we respond to potentially difficult situations. These situations may happen to us several times every day. Think about the angst and irritation you can build up, if you do not find alternative patterns for dealing with difficulties. The potential for conflict is also increased, leaving us in an anxious state, facing unresolved dilemmas. The same pattern of response plays out as clearly, and sometimes dramatically, in the workplace as it does in our personal lives.

Personal case study

Emma, an administrative section leader, described to me a typical scenario she had faced. After a difficult start to the day, at home with her 'stroppy' teenage daughter, and traffic jams en route, she was in no mood for dealing with others' 'unnecessary' issues and problems.

The first thing she heard as she entered the office was an answerphone message from one of her staff saying that she was ill and would not be in. Almost immediately she received a call from another member of staff, stating that she needed to take the day off to look after her young daughter, who was feeling unwell. She described this situation as typical amongst some of her staff and perceived that absenteeism was based often on minor problems and excuses [I noted that she had already made up her mind that this new situation was not a legitimate case!].

She described her thoughts, which were 'This is the last thing I need today,' 'She's done this before,' and 'This is one step too far!' She felt annoyed, irritated and frustrated. Her actual behavioural response was to ignore the request and insist that the person find a way of coming in. This resulted in a difficult telephone conversation followed by a period of confrontation in the office with a number of staff, and threats of a grievance procedure being invoked. She admitted that this pattern of her 'getting tough' response was becoming too frequent and had ramped up the levels of pressure both at work and home.

We explored an alternative route through this situation and what she could learn for similar experiences in the future.

Adopting a different perception based on the absence situation, rather than the person, and accepting that the sudden illness was true, it then provided a legitimate case for time off. She also recognised how much she was taking the effect of her problems with her daughter into her work relationships, especially with her team.

Powering Through Pressure

This change could then be supported by thinking along the lines of, 'I need to focus on dealing with what is actually happening and the consequences, rather than my feelings about the individuals involved.'

This was likely to result in feelings of concern, empathy and determination to tackle issues, as she encountered similar incidents in the future.

Finally, her actions would include acknowledging the person, checking out what she could do, contacting HR or a colleague, exploring options to fill the gaps, and positively following up with both people, on their return to work. She also recognised the difference that gaining her partner's support would make in working together to resolve some issues and get agreements with her daughter.

Activity

Take time now to consider situations where you adopt the more negative pathway or you are aware that there is a pattern that has led you to reduce your options or become fixed in your position.

What is your current perception of the situation?

What are your immediate thoughts about the people or situation?

How does this leave you feeling?

What are your unhelpful responses and what happens as a result, that may add further pressure for you and others?

Now identify an alternative, more productive pathway.

What are the facts of the situation? What is actually happening? In what ways could you perceive the situation more positively?

What constructive thoughts are you now having about the people and the situation?

Thinking in this way, what feelings are generated?

What is likely to be your productive responses and actions?

In summary, what does this tell you about what will help you to reduce the pressure on yourself when you get into a negative response pattern?

Thinking and feeling

Reliance on our thinking and logical perceptive processes plays a major part in other ways, which can increase or reduce the amount of pressure we experience.

Many people attempt to suppress and disregard their feelings in the workplace or separate them from their thinking, but this can be a mistake. You may have experienced this when you ignored your gut feelings or your intuitive sense and that has influenced your immediate reactions to what someone else has said or done. When we place less emphasis on our emotional responses, we can find it more difficult to deal satisfactorily with the anxieties resulting from the pressure. Yet, for many of us, it is not surprising that the effect on ourselves and others, which is based on these emotional responses, is what drives our final decisions and actions.

Making use of an appropriate combination of thinking and feeling can be one of the most critical skills in the workplace. Often this is referred to as emotional intelligence: those who can think clearly, expansively and analytically through situations and issues, then couple that ability with consideration of the impact of decisions on those affected. They usually produce the most powerful and comprehensive solutions.

Personal case study

Consider John, who seems totally reliant on a thinking response, who is likely to ignore important behaviour in others and who doesn't understand the importance of feelings in the workplace, or see them as relevant to getting work done. John finds it incredibly difficult to respond positively to, and deal with, any situations where others are under pressure, or have situations that are difficult for them. As a result, he is considered by some of his colleagues to be cold, detached, uncaring, lacking empathy and thick-skinned. So, despite being professionally competent and a convincing decision-maker, he is unable to get a strong level of commitment from others when he needs that extra effort on some of his project work. In fact, when he is under pressure and needs support, others rarely offer to help.

In contrast, Calum, John's colleague, is almost totally reliant on his gut feelings, his highly intuitive observations and his own emotional reactions to influence his responses. These approaches help him make decisions that he believes will be the best for everyone. At times he is unfocused, but can be critical of people who use data 'for their own ends', are interested only in 'bottom-line decision-making'. He believes that they do not consider the consequences of their decisions or actions. Some others perceive him as too open, wearing his heart on his sleeve, sometimes appearing flaky and often delaying decisions by too much consideration of all the parties' interests and his need to seek consensus.

As you can imagine, John and Calum do not get on well. John avoids him and leaves him out of important activities, whilst Calum often gets upset and can be resistant to John's plans. At some level they both know that they need to work together to achieve the outcomes expected.

What they both realised after a facilitated discussion was that they didn't have to agree with each other, be the best of friends or understand why they responded as they did. However, they could see that there was an enormous amount to be gained by recognising, valuing and making use of each other's strengths at different times. This produced better results and outcomes, often much more quickly. Another big spin-off was that the more they worked alongside each other, the more they learned to adopt each other's elements into their own working approach and style.

Activity

Ask yourself these questions:

Do you know people like John, or do you recognise some of yourself in his almost totally thinking-based approach to work?

How does this approach affect you and others?

What is the consequence for you when you use this approach?

Both thinking and feeling approaches have an essential part to play in generating and reducing pressure for ourselves and others, especially in situations where there is already tension and the potential for conflict. Combining the best of what we think and how we and others feel, often helps us to consider more options and reach higher quality solutions. Our thinking first will help us to focus on gathering the important facts, gather relevant information, analyse options and generate solutions. We can then take actions which consider the effect on people. This will mean that we are more likely to make sound judgements about how to support them and gain their commitment.

Many people use analytical thinking to avoid getting drawn into emotional games and to remain as neutral as possible. Combining this approach with considering the consequences of our decisions, and identifying how others can become engaged, will ensure that we are making decisions that both appeal to logical sense and are based on appreciation of others and their values. This is the critical step to getting commitment, reducing resistance and building support.

Drawing on our emotional intelligence, we learn more, make better assessments of situations, and have a stronger range of options available to manage the pressures we face.

Separating body and mind

Another often unhelpful form of separation involves us focussing on our physiology as being more important than consideration of our state of mind. This position also occurs frequently in the workplace.

Personal case study

When I met Tim, a finance specialist, he first told me that he thought he might be stressed because he was experiencing bursts of breathlessness, overtiredness, lack of energy and occasional soreness in his chest. He had seen his GP who had diagnosed high blood pressure and immediately arranged for a heart scan. After receiving clear scan results, he was prescribed blood pressure and sleeping tablets. Using this treatment, he noted a very slight shift in his symptoms. However, he was still perplexed by his ongoing nervous and physiological condition. Finally one of his colleagues referred him to me to see if we could consider any alternative approaches.

I asked about his work and life and a number of pressure triggers emerged:

→ He thought that his job was at risk with rumours of redundancy rife throughout the business and his role not being seen as a valuable central service.
→ He was concerned about his parents' health and was spending a lot of his time contacting and supporting them.

→ Concurrently, he was finding his relationship with his partner difficult, but they had not talked about what was happening or what he was experiencing. This lack of openness was further increasing his anxiety.

As you would imagine with that amount of pressure affecting him, it wasn't surprising, as we explored further, that he was anxious, fearful of several likely worst scenarios, and uncertain what he could do. He was 36, a time he associated with the need to be achieving in a responsible role, providing security for his family, and building confidence based on strong self-belief. At this time, he considered that he had none of these and his self-confidence was low.

Through a process of integrated coaching that considers the whole work/life picture, we discussed a range of options that would tackle the issues he was facing, rather than just focussing on and worrying about the physical signs of pressure. He decided to:

→ Share his family concerns with his siblings and ask them to take greater responsibility for their parents' situation.
→ Meet with his boss and an HR colleague to discuss his future, possible job options and re-training.
→ Talk immediately with his partner about his anxieties, condition and concerns, as well as understanding her position.

The result of these plans was that he and his partner had a very open discussion and decided how they would spend more time together, and communicate differently to share both their burdens. Likewise, once his siblings were aware of his parental concerns, they stepped up and took their share of the supportive care time. At work, an alternative position was identified by HR, and this offered greater future security and increased his sense of contribution and the significance of his role. Not surprisingly, there was an accompanying dramatic reduction in his physical symptoms, which stunned his GP on his next appointment.

Dealing with part of any difficult situation nearly always leaves some issues unresolved or only partially improved. The result is that we continue to experience the same pressures. By recognising and responding to the power of our emotions, and the importance of communicating these, we usually fully understand situations, others' positions and feel much closer to resolution.

It is okay to change your beliefs

Another way that we diminish the importance of our feeling state begins with some of the beliefs that we may hold about what is important and right at work.

There is an element of truth to all of these statements but, when they dominate our approach to dealing with pressure situations, we can generate additional internal strain through the way we behave, and develop habitual responses based on our own self-perception of what is right. This can produce a pattern of response that overrides other positive beliefs and the skills that make us successful.

Consider how the belief statements that are sitting like discs in your head can, when triggered, take over your behaviour. For example, if you believe that other people will not like it when you express your feelings, you are more likely to hold back from giving clear and honest feedback when someone has not done what you needed or expected from them. As a result, situations do not improve and your anxiety is likely to be increased.

There are times when we need to look at and challenge our own beliefs and understand how these play a role in increasing the pressure we are under. Where certain beliefs remain unchallenged, we can become constrained by our thinking and may be heading towards experiencing chronic stress patterns.

There is good news

There is an excellent framework that first helps us to understand our constraining beliefs and the resultant behaviour, then helps us to identify ways we can change these. It is a model that I have used consistently and had great personal and client success with. The process I use with clients begins by asking them to identify what is happening currently, using a structure that I call the 'Doom Loop'. This was a name triggered by one of my clients who said, 'I lose confidence in dealing with those people, and it feels like I'm descending into a dark hole full of doom and gloom.'

A negative belief cycle

The Doom Loop

Negative belief
I can't ...
I am no good at ...
It's difficult for me ...

Negative conformation
How do others respond?
What is my perception
of their feedback?

Internal reaction
What do I think and
feel as I approach
certain situations?

Performance disruption
How is my performance
affected in the situation?

Some of the most common examples I encounter, where this process works, are in areas such as feeling concerned about presenting to others, doing poorly in interviews, not dealing effectively with conflict, and difficulties experienced when negotiating with 'experts'. But it also kicks in, during all types of situations, where you feel a lack of confidence, experience low self-esteem, or are fearful about how you will perform in particular situations with specific people.

The typical doom loop presentation cycle begins with a message that we hold in our heads, based on a belief we have developed about our own competence, picked up and reinforced by past negative experiences. You might recognise messages that play out for you, such as, 'I am no good at presenting to groups,' 'I don't express myself clearly or strongly,' or 'They are so much more confident than I am.'

You will notice that the self-statements begin with phrases like, 'I'm not able to,' 'I can't,' 'I always struggle,' or 'They are ... I am not.' These beliefs, once activated, have already put us on a slippery slope of doubt and anxiety about how well we can do.

When people who have this belief are asked to give a presentation, or give their thoughts about a key issue, they begin to experience worrying thoughts and feelings. A wave of negative thoughts engulfs them, such as, 'This is so difficult,' or 'They are not interested in what I have to say.' This in turn generates feelings of anxiety, concern and worry. Together, their thoughts and feelings sweep across their consciousness. As a result, when they are approaching the situations that trigger this pattern, often they will experience internal reactions such as stomach upset, difficulty sleeping, forgetfulness and an inability to stay focussed.

Then, when they actually begin to present, suffering under this level of internal thinking pressure, often they will hurry their words or slow everything down to a crawl. They may also move about uncomfortably, lose contact with the audience, mumble or become hesitant when responding to others' questions.

What follows is a fixation with some of the responses and reactions from others. What we pick up will be interpreted as, 'He's looking annoyed, so I must be talking nonsense' or 'I'm not getting any questions or responses, so they are obviously not interested.'

This completes the cycle by confirming the initial beliefs and self-statements and reinforcing the message, 'I'm not a good presenter' or 'I can't express my ideas under pressure.'

For years, as a young employee, this process was very true for me when dealing with senior people who appeared to be so knowledgeable and competent. It dramatically affected my willingness to put myself into situations where I could make an impact and have my ideas listened to, despite having a lot of fresh ideas that others would have found useful. I found that, at its extreme, this type of cycle became debilitating, dramatically affecting my confidence.

The good news was that I discovered a cure, an alternative way of approaching, thinking and dealing with these situations that could take the place of my own Doom Loop. I now call this replacement process the 'Wow Loop'.

A positive belief cycle

The Wow Loop

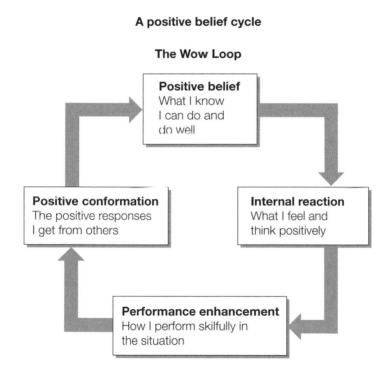

How this worked in those presentation situations where a belief triggered my nervous system into unproductive negative performance, was as follows.

First, I began to question and positively challenge the reality and truth of the beliefs I held and the recurring statements that played out on the disc in my head. It's often useful to involve others in supporting you with this. They are often better at telling you what you can do and are capable of, more easily than you are yourself.

You now will have a belief such as, 'I am good at coming up with new ideas,' supported by a positive premise, 'People want to know what I am thinking.' To get to this point, I learnt to think about situations in which I was particularly skilful or competent, or where I did present in ways that produced positive responses and outcomes.

These self-reinforcing statements are referred to often as affirmations and, as such, at first can be difficult to accept. We may need to repeat the messages a number of times before we accept them as valid. Writing them down or putting them in a place you often visit, such as your diary or notebook system, will provide a continuously helpful reminder. I remember a time when I put positive statements on a lot of yellow sticky labels, which were placed strategically around the house. My family found it amusing to encounter these statements in the fridge, on the bathroom mirror and on the car dashboard. Each time I read one, it made me smile, which reinforced the positivity of the message. It is important that you find your best way of ensuring you can see or hear a supportive message, when you most need it.

The next step involves getting yourself in the best possible state as you approach a situation that may trigger anxiety. One way of building your strength is to carry out rigorous preparation of your goals, approach and style for this situation. When we know our material, most of us are more confident. Testing out our approach or presentation on others we trust will help us to know our way around the content and enable us to get supportive feedback. Another way we can help ourselves is by allowing sufficient time to prepare. Rushing from a meeting into a presentation is never the best way of putting yourself into a healthy energetic state.

Many successful people also use positive visioning to generate a strong sense of what success will be like when they have performed at their best. This helps them to focus on getting it right. This activity can involve simply taking several minutes before you start to think about what you are like and what you are professionally doing on that day, when you will perform at your best. Then imagine getting affirmative responses that will show you what you are doing to achieve the results you want. Finally, having a way of relaxing and breathing deeply and effectively will put you in a strong and more relaxed physical state.

Powering Through Pressure

You are now in the situation and it's at this point that you draw on your resilience, particularly your known skills and expertise. You know what good looks like, so you sit and stand professionally, breathe deeply and make eye contact with the people who matter. Create an anchor point for yourself, whether that's a secure seated position, a table to rest your notes on or coming forward to a spot where you can engage easily with others. Now you will find that you are able to deliver with clarity, being concise and using firmness to show that you are serious. As you deliver, having already identified what a successful response will be like, you look for these in your audience. Questions, enquiries seeking to understand more, agreement on key points, others building on your ideas and their commitments to action, are all examples of your presentation working. I often choose a friendly face to focus on who I know will accurately show what is working by their response.

Finally, carry out your own review, focussing on what has worked and what you have achieved. The results and outcomes you achieve reinforce your now imbedded positive belief and this is the one that will be triggered in future presentation scenarios.

This process replaces a negative cycle that you recognise is no longer needed or useful with a positive one that enables you to continue performing successfully. Having someone who will coach you through this process often adds a valuable dimension.

Today I present to all manner of groups with only slight nerves. These I recognise are essential to keep me on my toes, and the different belief, thoughts, feelings, skills and feedback reinforce the message, 'I do present my ideas well.'

Summary

In this chapter we have explored the importance of using your thinking and your feelings together as emotional intelligence, to enable you to have a range of appropriate responses in order for you to deal with pressure situations.

Using the immediate response model, you have learnt that to understand and act in a positive way will help, particularly when negativity is creating additional pressure for you in your dealing with others.

Do you tend to separate your physical and your emotional state, which in turn stops you from detecting and interpreting the whole range of symptoms, based on the most important issues you face, when you are under pressure? Learning to read the emotional and intellectual signs often will provide alternative clues as to your best ways of preventing stress.

Finally, the 'Doom Loop' provides a way of understanding the process that you go through when you struggle with a particular type of situation or work activity. A much better alternative uses the tactics evident in the 'Wow Loop', to replace a potentially debilitating pattern with a highly resourceful one.

The more you understand your whole self and make maximum use of all your internal resources and skills, the more you will have appropriate and integrated strategies in place to tackle most of the issues and problems you face.

Maturity is the ability to think, speak and act your feelings within the bounds of dignity.
SAMUEL ULLMAN

Addressing relationships that aren't working

> ## Personal relationships are the fertile soil from which all advancement, all success, all achievement in real life grows. BEN STEIN

In my research and throughout my client work, the greatest source of pressure on many occasions has come from the difficulties and anxiety that we associate with managing certain 'difficult' relationships. All of us have experienced aggressive bosses or senior managers, a raft of over demanding or uncooperative colleagues, and staff who constantly drain our energy. If a pressurised encounter with these people happens on a regular basis, we soon choose the 'easy' options, give in, give way, give up or leave. If we can improve some of these relationships and take actions sooner, then we can reduce our pressure levels dramatically and, at the same time, increase our job satisfaction and, ultimately, our overall performance.

Personal case study

Martin was an experienced member of a very busy office team, who was faced with a growing number of people at work who, he claimed, did not understand him, appreciate his approach or value his contribution. He considered that his boss expected an enormous amount of him by delegating 'too much too often', usually with short timescales. For someone who liked to take his time, and was a perfectionist at heart, this created a constant state of anxiety. I particularly remember his saying, 'What if I make mistakes by hurrying and do not check properly?' He described his colleagues also as tending to take advantage of his goodwill, frequently asking for his help and interrupting with questions when he needed to concentrate on the task at hand. Recently he had been asked to mentor a couple of new staff and, although he enjoyed sharing his expertise and knowledge, he was critical of their lack of application and the expectation that he would solve their problems for them.

This had left him tired, frustrated and increasingly off-hand with a wide range of people. He had been 'criticised' also by his manager for his negative attitude and not being a team player.

What especially struck me was the cumulative effect of the demands that he faced daily, coming from all directions. He had also developed negative assumptions about others' attitudes and he was concerned about taking too strong action. He was convinced that it was 'their fault' and it was not his approach that was the problem!

After a long discussion teasing out the facts of the situation, he agreed to check with others as to the extent that their version of events matched his. Surprisingly for him, they all agreed how much they appreciated his experience, admitted they may have taken him for granted and agreed that they had become over-reliant on his input. Because he never complained or raised his concerns, they assumed he was okay with their approach and the workload he 'willingly' assumed.

Having opened up the situation, Martin soon found that he was able to discuss and agree what was acceptable at the time, thereby encouraging others to be more flexible and aware of his pressures, at that point. The support for him that followed this change, and his new-found confidence by being assertive when demands became too great, provided a very different and increasingly positive set of relationships going forward. His role as a mentor became a massive strength within his group and a great self-motivator.

Our stories and the different stories of others

Like Martin, we all have our stories about others and these have been built up often over a considerable period of time to the point where they may be so far removed from the actual truth. These perceptions unfortunately dominate our position concerning the situation, and drive our intentions. This in turn guides our specific behaviour and the way we respond to those people.

Where our version of events and situations come from

The first step in dealing with a situation where there is a strong emotional element, with very different perceptions, is to recognise what our story is and how 'inaccurate' it has become. These inaccuracies can represent:

→ **Our first impressions** 'I knew as soon as I met him we were not going to get on, he was so arrogant.' 'She's just like my sister, never thinking before she speaks.'
→ **Our biases** 'As a typical techie, he's never attempted to understand my needs. ▶

He only tells us what we should do in language only they can understand.'
'You can't trust HR.'

→ **Our stereotypes** 'As an information systems person, she hasn't a clue about running a business.' 'He's a typical British manager; won't get to the point and talks in circles.'

→ **Our values** 'Her black-and-white, take-it-or-leave-it attitude makes me sick.' 'He can't see at all that you have to work hard for a long time to earn money.'

→ **Our generalisations** 'She always looks down her nose at me and is never wrong.' 'Every day he moans about exactly the same old things.'

→ **Our exaggerations** 'The whole issue is down to him, and he's impossible to deal with.' 'Her spelling mistakes are appalling and could bring all of us down.'

→ **Our history** 'She has been a constant thorn in my side and undermined my position regularly in front of our clients. It's got worse since I was promoted and she wasn't.' 'Two years ago he did the same thing. It's become a really nasty pattern.'

Inevitably, when we get the opportunity to hear from the other party, their story is very different, and, of course, tainted by their own particular sources. It is not surprising that we may make decisions to go no further in our attempts to resolve some of the deep-seated relationship problems. Most of these elements carry strongly negative emotional reactions, with deep fears and pain that strongly influence our current behaviour and responses, thus maintaining our anxiety.

I now remember, with some embarrassment, working with a new colleague with whom I verbally competed for a long time. What I didn't realise was that the level of interaction quite quickly moved from 'humorous' sparring to barbed criticism, then into attack and, ultimately, to direct abuse. It was resolved only when our boss threatened to lock us in a room until we found some way of talking about what was happening and agreed how we would behave differently. For the first time, united by the same personal goal, we spoke with honesty and became increasingly aware of how far our biased take on the other person had deteriorated and our accompanying behaviour had intensified. Neither of us wanted to continue in the same way, and both of us demonstrated a willingness to understand the other person and find some common ground.

By challenging the basis of our perceptions, we can all rethink situations and, as part of this essential change, encourage others to reconsider their position as well. From the examples used in the following table, notice what a powerful role the language we use plays in adding an emotional intensity.

The basis of our perception	Means of challenging what is said
The influence of first impressions	'What have I/you noticed that is different or has changed?'
Biases	'What do they contribute that is valuable and helpful?'
Stereotypes	'In what ways are they different from the norm?'
Values	'What values do you share?'
Generalisations	'Always? Never? Totally?'
Exaggerations	Question the extent, e.g. 'How much/ important is…?'
History	Focus on the present and moving forward, 'What can he do now and what can he contribute as things develop?'

I have to struggle to change people's perceptions of me. I grew very frustrated with the perception that I'm this shy, retiring, inhibited aristocratic creature when I'm absolutely not like that at all. I think I'm much more outgoing and exuberant than my image. HELENA BONHAM CARTER

Having difficult conversations

Having recognised that our story is only a version or part of our way of dealing with a difficult situation, and admitted that others may have a skewed but equally viable version, we now need to find a way of conducting a dialogue, which will enable us to develop fresh thinking and agree positive actions. I use the word dialogue deliberately because it conveys these essential elements.

Adopting a positive dialogue
→ Willingness to clearly articulate our position.

→ Control over our stronger, emotionally loaded behaviour.

→ Being prepared to listen to what they have to say without interruption.

→ Seeking to understand what is behind their story and what is not being said.

→ Focusing on what needs to be different and can change.

→ Aiming towards workable solutions for both parties.

This change is not easy but will prove essential if both of you are to move from your previously biased positions.

A structure that I have found very useful to follow, and have used on many occasions, is one I adapted from the work of Marshall Rosenberg, a world-renowned mediator, negotiator and facilitator. The process stresses the need to use all four critical parts, to uncover what we both believe and what is important for us both.

My position and story	Others' position and story
What is my perception of the situation and what has happened?	What is your perception of the situation and what has happened?
What effect has this situation had on me?	What effect has this situation had on you?
What need do I have that is not being met?	What need of yours is not being met?
What am I prepared to offer to do?	What are you prepared to offer to do?

This works in practice first by stating **what has happened so far** in neutral, factually accurate terms. This requires you to use language that is non-blaming and not based on assumptions and guesses.

A typical example I have heard is, 'When I am speaking in the management meeting, you sometimes cut across me before I have finished and usually you introduce different thinking before we can explore and discuss my ideas.' I can encourage the other person by asking them what their understanding of our situation is and what has happened.

As a second step, we need to be able to state **the effect that the behaviour or actions has had on us**, and what has followed. This description needs to sound non-blaming or it is likely you will provoke a negative response. Building on the situation above, this could be expressed as, 'When this happens I am left feeling deflated and frustrated, usually resulting in my pushing back strongly or sometimes ignoring your views. This often leads to an argument in front of our colleagues, by which I'm embarrassed.' This type of statement, as well as letting others know the effect they are having, also acknowledges our responsibility for our feelings and reactions. In order to encourage the other person, a good question is, 'How does that affect you?' or 'What is the outcome for you?' Other examples you may encounter are:

→ 'When you take over the activity, I'm left feeling disappointed and am reluctant to get involved.'

→ 'We agreed what would happen and you have not followed through. I'm left feeling unvalued and that this work doesn't matter to you.'

→ 'Several times I've produced work, which you have presented as your efforts. This can result in my not trusting you.'

The third stage requires us to identify **needs**, including values, desires and expectations that are not being met, for either of us. Rosenberg describes this as the point of breakthrough that will tell us what needs to change for us both to feel positive. Although not common for many of us, identifying needs will allow us also to focus on 'getting it right' rather than dwelling on what is wrong. This is because usually we associate our needs as being at a deeper level than the perceived thoughts and feelings.

We also share some of the most important needs, such as trust, respect, appreciation, support and truth-telling. So, if we can find commonality here, then it is likely to provide a real desire in us both to resolve the situation. It can be helpful at this stage to ask the other person first about their needs that can be met, as it shows regard for really understanding what is important to them in the situation, e.g. 'What do you need to happen?' 'What is missing for you?' 'What do you want to be different?'

Our statement could be something like, 'I need to be listened to and given space to develop my ideas without interruption in that meeting. This is important to build others' respect and my credibility.'

The final part involves statements of **what we are prepared to do** to move forward with the situation or **what we may wish to request** of the other person. Again, it can be productive for you to ask first what the other person is willing to do, or make an offer with an action that you are willing to take, e.g. 'I am willing to speak with you before the meetings and bring you into the discussion as soon as I've explained my idea.' 'Are you willing to check with me before you come into the discussion?'

I have developed a summary check process that you could include at the end of the discussion, to summarise what has been covered, where you are now with the issue and what has been agreed. Alternatively, you could ask them the following questions to check their understanding:

→ What are your/my thoughts now about the situation?
→ How does this leave our relationship?
→ How will we ensure we follow through?
→ What else do we need to talk about or do?
→ Who else is affected by our agreements?
→ Who do we want to involve or inform?

Using language based on 'we' and 'us' encourages both people to think in terms of joint agreement and collective action.

This process for tackling difficult issues, and the sequence described here, has worked just as well in my personal life as it has in tackling work-relationship issues. Given the emotional intensity that can be experienced in this context, my family and friends can all attest to its validity!

Dealing with 'bad' bosses

When I looked at the information given by people as they left to get away from a problematic job, the reason most often given was about 'the behaviour of my boss'. If you have worked for someone who you labelled as a 'bad boss', you will have experienced considerable pressure, sometimes over a long period of time. So what can you do to manage upwards, bring about change and reduce that pressure?

In the research, the most common ways that managers generate pressure for others, even though in many cases they are not aware of the effect they are having, is:

→ **Aggressive behaviour** Many managers are not aware of the impact that their behaviour is having on their people. So until it is raised generally they will continue in the same vein. This can include harassment, bullying, dismissing or ignoring and being over-critical.

→ **Making excessive demands and expectations** In these days of high targets and demanding goals, many managers consider that it is appropriate to raise expectations continuously. Given this occurs often in situations where resources have been reduced, this level of expectation will then be considered unfair, unjust and excessive.

→ **Modelling 'Long hours syndrome'** There are large numbers of managers who, in order to get their own work done, now stretch their working day. This practice is then informally adopted by their staff as the normal standard, and their working hours quickly become extended. This results in demotivation and frustration.

→ **Providing insufficient information** Sometimes managers feel that they have to keep information to themselves or withhold it to 'protect' their staff. That is fine except where it prevents them from doing the job they need to do. It can also create uncertainty when others believe they are being excluded or key information is deliberately being withheld.

→ **Unwillingness to appropriately delegate and coach** There are mangers who believe that the only people who can do the job to the standard required are themselves. With this attitude they create an excessive workload for themselves and do not develop others or provide opportunities in order for them to learn and achieve a better standard.

→ **Micro-managing** Linked to the previous attitude, there are a high number of managers who think they will be in control only if they know everything and stay involved in all that is happening. As a result, they get immersed consistently in detailed checking and monitoring, which creates a sense of constantly being observed and a lack of trust.

→ **Shortage of resources and necessary support** Under the pressure to keep costs down, managers often make the decision to reduce headcount and tighten equipment, technology and time constraints across the board. Most people do not like to work in a job where they do not have the appropriate level of resources to do a good job. Any under-resourcing from cut-backs will put a strain on those who remain.

→ **Inconsistency of approach** Pressure is generated, particularly within close-working teams, where there is a perception that the manager is treating different people in different ways. This is then judged by the staff to be unfair, biased or prejudicial. Usually it encourages members to play politics in order to remain in favour.

→ **Non-delivery of what has been promised** When staff believe that certain things have been promised or agreed and then the manager fails to deliver what was expected, it creates a lack of trust. If this happens on a number of occasions then extra pressure is generated, especially during times of change.

→ **Playing politics** Within organisations many people believe that playing politics is one of the key attributes to becoming successful in that culture. It is helpful, and at times essential, to understand how things work and how to get things done. However, when bosses focus on being seen in the right places, with the right people, deliberately and manipulatively cultivating certain relationships, it breeds distrust of those managers' motives. This leads to people expending energy by worrying what to do and how to do the 'right' things involving the 'right' people.

For many of these challenges, there are some typically helpful ways that you can use to influence what your bosses are doing or not doing.

1   Give feedback in a way that is specific and positioned as a reasonable request rather than a threat. Using 'I need [support/information/time/resources/coaching] from you' often is better received than 'I want …'

2   Raise the issue as a concern, and state the effect it is having on you and or others, for example, 'When you cancel the critical customer update meeting at short notice, it reduces the response I can make to the client, as I don't have current data.'

3   Check out how accurate your perceptions are, based on their actual statements of expectation and actions, 'When you said that I was responsible, what did you specifically mean, and what activities were you referring to?' Many managers fail to be explicit about how they want roles to be carried out and this can be an issue when staff think that they have the freedom to act as a real part of delegated responsibility.

4   When you are not getting clarity, state what you need in order to do a good job: 'If I am going to hit that deadline, I need the guidelines/input/information/outline from you before the end of the day.'

5   If you don't know, or don't have sufficient information, ask for it: 'You can help me to respond to that customer by writing a context statement. You have the best overview of what we are hoping to achieve.'

6   Check out whether your perception of the situation matches that of other people whose judgement you trust. Is the behaviour of your manager aimed only at you? Are others experiencing similar situations or have they encountered negatives in the past?

7   Be willing to negotiate over what is achievable and possible, especially where there are resource constraints, involving support, finance, technology or time: 'I am prepared to give extra time if you free me from the group meeting. Will you also coach me on different ways of writing those documents?'

8   If the behaviour of a boss is developing into a pattern that may involve harassment or bullying, you have the right to raise the issue

with the appropriate person, often a senior manager or human resources advisor, without it putting your job at risk. The term 'new managerial bully' has come into vogue in a range of circumstances. Usually it refers to managers who respond to the pressure they are under by then behaving aggressively towards their staff. You do not have to tolerate such behaviour and have an absolute right to raise it with your senior staff or through a grievance process.

These ideas apply equally to relationships with 'difficult' colleagues, clients and suppliers. What is most important is that we recognise that we have the right to raise concerns, give feedback and make requests of others, when we encounter unacceptable behaviour. It is particularly important when it is creating more pressure than is necessary. Until we do these things on a regular basis, others will continue to behave in the same ways, and the pressures we face will continue and grow.

As a manager, what about the pressure that comes from your team?

Personal case study

Let me describe three of 'the staff from hell', as experienced and described by their manager, Michael, when we met. In his words, they all contributed to growing pressure on him, in very different ways.

George was an 'old stager' who had a set way of doing things: resisted change at all cost, refused to 'go the extra mile' and had no time for the number of young 'upstarts' now in the team. Often he had a rant at Harry and was critical of Jez behind his back.

Harry kept his head down, worked whenever possible by himself, said nothing in meetings, and was often sour when asked to take on new or team activities. He kept out of the way of George and found himself drawn into arguments and then taking sides with Jez.

Jez was overly confident, appeared full of himself, despite his lack of experience, often presented completely new processes for introduction and regularly sounded off about the performance of others who 'were not pulling their weight' or 'were past it'. This was aimed primarily at George, and he strongly influenced Harry to agree with him.

If this sounds like a vipers' nest, it was for Michael, who had not been a manager for very long and was struggling to maintain a semblance of order and levels of productivity.

What we discussed and agreed is typical of what many managers need to do to get on top of difficult staff situations, where those involved seem to have the power to create and put energy into negativity rather than positive team action.

Michael and I explored the complex set of relationships and the effect they were creating collectively. This resulted in some powerful realisations and he agreed to:

→ involve his manager in jointly tackling the team atmosphere issues and to ensure that he did things 'by the book'. This manager had not realised how difficult Michael was finding his situation and wanted to support him to make a success of his role.

→ meet with each individual separately to discuss performance and behaviour concerns and to restate his expectations about what were acceptable standards. We discussed his need to identify the benefits for each individual, to enlist their cooperation and to have thought through the actions he was prepared to take if he did not get agreement or compliance. Each individual was somewhat surprised, but was willing to listen to Michael's position and they were all able to negotiate some opportunities that would meet specific needs. Michael decided to make greater use of the experience and ideas coming from all three staff in a key joint task, which made use of their different strengths.

→ finally, he decided to use an experienced colleague as a coach and mentor, to support him as he progressed through the next few weeks, particularly in reinforcing and sustaining the changes the staff had agreed to make.

He also realised he needed to respond to unsatisfactory performance issues sooner, undergo training on some core management skills and build in the support of other members of his team, to help him to tackle the team culture issues.

What he gained most was the realisation that he did not need to tackle everything himself in order to establish himself as a credible manager. Using the support around him and involving others in setting standards proved critical to his sustaining the change.

Summary

In this chapter you have been able to understand a number of different ways that people experience the pressure created in relationships, particularly at work. Hopefully you now know that you will always have a choice about how you respond to these situations. This realisation about always having choice, when the behaviour of others adds pressure, is such a powerful reinforcement and enabler of change.

Activity

Consider these questions in relation to your current work relationships:

Which relationships are working well for you?

What do you do to get these to work?

Which relationships are creating pressure for you?

What are others doing that is contributing to this pressure?

You may well have considered these situations, in the light of whether there was a big difference in thinking about each other and the 'truth' of the situation.

It is also important that you realise when you have very different stories about other people. Think about how these stories have developed. Is it from stereotypes, biases or aspects of your personal history with that person? Finally, you have considered what you can do to improve difficult relationships, whether that is as a manager of others or in response to the person you report to.

The four key points on dealing with relationship issues in order to reduce pressure are:

→ Be clear about what you expect from others.

→ Catch difficult situations early.

→ Identify where your stories about others may be skewed and how they affect your behaviour and response to them.

→ Use different approaches to tackle different people and first focus on how you can meet each other's needs.

> I believe in businesses where you engage in creative thinking, and where you form some of your deepest relationships. If it isn't about the production of the human spirit, we are in big trouble. ANITA RODDICK

Feeling good about change

Chapter Six

If you don't like something, change it. If you can't change it, change your attitude. MAYA ANGELOU

In a world that is constantly changing, we judge our achievements often by our ability to be able to deal with the way that we are affected by change and the extent that we can influence what happens to us. So this capability has become a critical life and work skill. Consequently, it is an arena that generates an enormous amount of work and personal pressure.

To reduce pressure throughout a period of transition, first you may need to be more willing to adopt a positive way of thinking about what is changing, which then will influence your responses. Our thinking about change tends to mean that we are more likely to fall into one of two incredibly different camps: those we can identify as acceptors/responders and those who can be perceived as resistors/opposers.

Activity

Ask yourself this question:

Of these thinking positions, which would you naturally associate with or recognise in others around you?

Place yourself along each continuum, based on what you currently think about change.

Change is unnecessary .... We need change

Change always causes problems .... Change creates opportunities

Change is costly .... Change generates income

Change is awful .... Change is wonderful

Change is frightening .... Change is exciting

Change destroys my past learning .... Change enables me to learn afresh

I don't like any change .... I love change

Change needs to be resisted .... Change needs to be embraced

Right now I need stability .... Right now I need change

I am more often a:

Resistor/Opposer .... **Acceptor/Responder**

Powering Through Pressure

If you find yourself associating more with the statements on the left side, then it is likely that you will find change difficult to accept or see the positive benefits that may result. Also you will limit the choices available to you, in the way that you respond. I am an advocate of being able to cast a challenging or questioning eye over change. Too many changes I have experienced or worked on have been ill thought through and have questionable validity. However, reliance on thinking that is biased towards making critical judgements, pessimism about success and general negativity, will always raise doubts, concerns and anxieties for you and others. Hopefully you now realise that this is the perfect route to add pressure internally, often at a time when there is already sufficient external pressure acting upon us. Admit it, or at least get used to the reality: change happens!

If you are a manager, it is essential that you have developed the skills necessary to be able to lead by positive example during change initiatives and to demonstrate constructive thinking and behaviour that supports the benefits and gains from the change.

Personal case study

Mike, an experienced sales manager, was expected to support the structural changes set out by his boss, as part of a drive to encourage new product development and sales. This would mean changing the roles for some of his team. He was not sure whether this was a good move and was concerned that some of his experienced people would be really annoyed and frustrated. This was the third reorganisation within the sales group, within a 15-month period!

When we met he was in a state of indecision and anxiety. Doing little except expressing his concerns, this was adding to his and others' doubts and reservations. We discussed the effect his response was likely to be having on his team, and eventually he recognised the need for him to take a stronger lead. He was reacting to the change very personally and had lost sight of the overall situation, and the potential gains and benefits available to many of the individuals in his team. If he could get these people on board, then there was a greater chance that they would influence the other doubters.

This approach worked better than he had imagined and, in a short period, he was able to spend time with and turn around those who were more negative. He focussed on listening to their concerns, coaching them to develop their

▶

skills, exploring options and encouraging them to adopt different thinking and approaches. These combined strategies increased their chances of discovering ways to make their new situation work, in their favour.

So Mike planned an approach that provided up-to-date, relevant information, demonstrated clear benefits and built in support when it was needed. By consistently repeating these elements, most of Mike's team accepted, at some level, that the changes were inevitable, they would all be affected and there were choices about the way that they responded and acted going forward. Most importantly, his openness and the time he dedicated to listening and firmly restating the key steps eventually swayed even the most resistant cynics.

One of the tools I regularly use in my coaching and leadership work, that was of considerable help to Mike and his team, is a framework originally developed by Elisabeth Kübler-Ross. It was derived from her work supporting people through trauma or dealing with the stressful effects of major life changes. This model has since been adapted into the business context, where it is now found to accurately represent the response of people to change, in a whole range of situations.

The change response curve

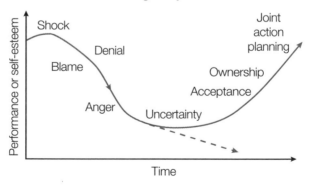

I have found that having a framework for dealing with transitions can be essential, especially when the effect of change has an impact far greater than we expect. There was a period in my life when I was probably in my best health state. I then embarked on an avalanche of change that shook me to my core. Within a six-week period I changed jobs into a different organisation, we moved house and my wife had a baby.

Any one of these life events is often enough to generate considerable strain, so combining three had the potential to catapult us into a chronic stress state. In my naivety I wondered why I was so tired, struggling to learn in my new role, and so easily irritable and impatient. This, despite these being changes that were so positive. There were times when it felt like we were going around in circles, failing to make progress and small issues were becoming major concerns.

Fortunately, a white knight appeared, not a financial guru but a wonderful coach, who introduced me to a set of insights that enabled me to appreciate and accept what was happening, and provided ways out of my downward spiral. He started by talking through the 'change response curve'. Sometimes we just need to understand that our responses to the effect of change follow a normal pathway and we can all move through the 'difficult' phases into productive activity.

I have adapted and continued to use this framework in all of my personal and client change work.

The model could provide a starting point for you to identify where you and others are during a period of change, by making use of the responses that you and they are demonstrating. What I have added are suggestions for managers and colleagues, so that you know how best to support others, as the changes evolve. You will recognise some of the responses from your own experiences, perhaps most vividly from ones that have involved powerful emotional, personal change.

When change is first announced, the immediate response is often one of **shock**. You will hear people say, 'OMG, what is happening?' These exclamations often are accompanied by a rise in energy, an increase in activity and even performance improvements.

Response point two is labelled **denial**. Here you will hear, 'It's no big deal,' or 'It won't affect me.' This usually indicates that people are not attaching much importance to the change or its potential impact on them. This reaction initially can be helpful to support and sustain business as usual but, most often through disassociation, will lead to people ignoring what is really occurring and its importance to them.

Response point three involves two forms of **blame**. The first is aimed at criticising others, those thought to be the protagonists who are totally responsible for the effects of the change. You will notice comments like, 'If only they had done more about ...' or 'Why didn't they inform us sooner?' This is followed often by an attack on self, characterised by declarations of, 'If only I had seen this coming,' 'I'll be totally out of my depth,' or 'Why didn't I do something about it months ago?' At this point individuals are taking too large a degree of responsibility for the change and its effect.

What usually follows is a burst of righteous **anger** aimed at anyone who might have contributed to the situation we now find ourselves in. It may represent a sense of increasing powerlessness to influence circumstances.

And then we descend into the slough of **uncertainty**, hopelessness and confusion. At its worst we may experience shut down, withdrawal or periods of staying in one place, doing nothing. Generally this reflects that we are either being overwhelmed by the range of choices and volume of information or we are feeling lost, not knowing what to do to make a difference. Sometimes this is referred to as a freeze or stuck state, and is accompanied by statements like, 'I just don't know what to do any more,' or 'I'm so unsure about what's happening.'

As the situation evolves, and hopefully with continued support from others, we experience increasingly positive signs of a thinking and behavioural shift, which can dramatically reduce the amount of anxiety and pressure we have faced. A first point of real hope is referred to as **acceptance**, which shows that we have realised that, practically, things are now different and we have observed that some people are moving forward and are achieving success.

There is now a time when our reactions reflect that we have taken **ownership** and accepted some responsibility for the way we choose to deal with the new situation. We demonstrate through our attitude and behaviour that it is up to us to make the best of the future and to influence its course.

Continued forward progress and growing optimism will mean that we actively seek out opportunities to work with others, **joint action planning**, to solve problems, deal with challenges and put energy into ways of sustaining progress.

You may now recognise this process as it has unfolded during these typically important change experiences.

Work	Personal
Change of company ownership	Break up of a relationship
Move into a new role or promotion	Becoming a parent
Change in your work base or station	Moving house or refurbishment
Introduction of new guidelines or processes	Dealing with benefits or claims
Taking on challenging activities	Learning a completely new activity
A new boss or team	Financial difficulties

On a daily basis, I hear people railing against the changes to which they are subjected. A common catch cry is, 'Oh, here we go again, yet another change! We haven't got over the last one.' Have you become one of those people who cannot accept the need and value for all of us to adapt, change and develop flexible skills? If so, consider the following positive responses and actions that could overcome those drivers or blocks that are most relevant for you, at each stage of the change process.

→ **Shock** Make the most of the energy that is generated to spur you and others on to greater efforts. Refer back to this energy when you lose momentum, at a later stage.

→ **Denial** Accept that it is okay to question the validity of the change, and the effect it is having on you. It is not okay to stay with your head buried in the sand and pretend it will go away.

→ **Blaming yourself** View being tough on yourself as part of the need to 'up your game' and maintain high standards. Recognise that staying in this place will only lower your confidence and reduce your self-esteem.

→ **Blaming and getting angry with others** 'They' probably deserve some criticism for the way things have been done so far, but it is better for you to channel your feelings towards the people who can make a difference through your use of constructive feedback. Ensure you have an outlet for rising anger, such as physical activity or throwing yourself into a project that will influence or change the things you are angry about.

- → **Uncertainty** It is reasonable to do nothing for a short time. Closing down is your way of protecting yourself and can allow you emotionally, intellectually and physically to sit still and recover, as a necessary respite. Forcing it all to make sense generally doesn't help. Neither will joining others in their uncertainty be of value as it will bring you all down.

- → **Acceptance** This is a profound step, usually achieved by recognising that things just happen, that change is inevitable and that there are possible gains and alternative options.

- → **Ownership** Taking some level of responsibility provides you with a sense of power, some control and more choice regarding how you deal with what is happening and what you will do to influence the future.

- → **Joint action planning** Joining others by seeking and offering support, will enable you to deal with any ongoing setbacks, resolve issues and make better choices about ways of sustaining the change so that it continues to work for you.

How best to help others through a change

Personal case study

Stella had been involved in several promotions in a short space of time. Just as she became more accustomed to one role, she was catapulted into a new scenario with a new team to lead. This cumulative pressure generated by constant change was beginning to take its toll on her personal state and, consequently, was affecting the way she managed her people. The signs that all was not well included her increasingly frequent mood swings, not picking up on her own and others' mistakes as they occurred, becoming more critical and inconsistent in the way she treated some individuals, and taking much longer to make decisions.

As we spoke she identified some of the things that had happened which were not indicative of her usual way of working. She had become withdrawn, which had resulted in her not using the available resources around her, and was self-critical for not being 'on the mark' with performance. She recognised that her own loss of focus and, in her eyes, 'poor performance' was affecting the behaviour, morale and productivity of her team.

The key changes that she made were to focus on what her team needed at that particular time, keep them better informed, and involve them as much as possible in the process of change. She also set up new agreements with the whole team about how they needed to work with and support each other. Her efforts were now aligned with those of her team and she had a process where everyone took responsibility for tracking changes and dealing with issues.

If you are a manager, you have an absolute responsibility to ensure that your people are provided with the resources, information, skills and support to have the best chance of making change work. My top 10 ways of doing this during a period of change are:

1 **Communicate like never before** Most people feel reassured and more trusting if they are given information that they believe to be relevant. It is an incorrect assumption that you have to protect your people and tell them as little as possible. Ask them, 'What do you need to know?' If at all possible, give them the best answer that you have.

2 **Have your awareness antennae on high alert** Many people have developed a cloaking mechanism that is aimed at not showing concern and anxiety. So you have to be on alert, spotting the small signs and checking out what they mean. If you are so caught up in your own worries, you will miss the telltale indicators of their growing pressure.

3 **Accept that different people move through the change process at different paces** Making decisions about, and behaving in the same way towards everyone may seem to be consistent, yet you know that different individuals will need very different forms and levels of support from you and others.

4 **Provide for or conduct coaching in any areas where individuals may find it difficult to cope** Pinpoint the areas which are likely to undermine individuals' confidence and pre-empt their growing concern by ensuring they become knowledgeable and skilful in those specific areas that will make a positive difference.

5 **Provide an outlet for negative feelings** Perhaps the Japanese businesses that provide rooms, objects and practices for letting off

steam have it right. If these are not available you may need to be the conduit for them to release their tension. Be prepared for some to cry, shout and laugh outrageously. They don't need you to join in, but what they will need from you, is understanding and empathy.

6 **Recognise and reward short-term success** When people are feeling low and more negative, it makes a difference when others recognise their efforts and go out of their way to respond positively to the progress they make and the successes, however small, they achieve. Regular appreciation needs to become a rule during uncertain and turbulent times.

7 **Identify best practice that your people will value as representing meaningful success** When our world appears to be crumbling about us, we need to find answers, fresh thinking and success in others that we can aspire to and emulate. Getting it right provides the means for others to see that there really is a way out of the jungle.

8 **Watch out for overload with certain individuals** You will have some people who rise to the challenge of change and take on anything that comes their way. Whatever their motives, they may become a godsend for you and it will be easy to take their efforts for granted. Remember, they will keep going and remain ravenous for more work, as long as their mind and body will stand up. When they drop, it will be too late! Encourage them to help and coach others to deal with things for themselves, rather than trying to do everything.

9 **Make tough choices** During change, most managers will want to remain as considerate of others for as long as possible, often tolerating what are not usually acceptable standards of work and behaviour. When you have done all you can, there will be times when you will need to make some tough decisions about some people and situations. You have enough going on without having to carry people who, despite all your best efforts, are not willing to move. At this point either they need external help or you may need to find the best way of letting them go.

10 **Model positive attitudes and behaviour** Whether you believe it or not, many of your people absolutely will look to you and other managers for guidance on what is the best way of dealing with

Powering Through Pressure

the changes. This includes responding positively and promoting what is needed for the team and business to continue to run most effectively. When you feel at your most vulnerable or emotionally wrecked, you will need to look into your deepest reservoirs of resilience and draw on what you know works when things are tough. You will have battled through all sorts of threats, problems, issues and traumas in your life, yet you are still there and in reasonable shape, considering what you are facing. Keep telling yourself and others that you can do what is needed as you've done it all before.

Remember WIFM (What's in It For Me). Our need to experience specific gains for embracing change will play a major part in the acceptance of change and our willingness to put effort into supporting it. If you are uncertain when you are confronted by a negative or pessimistic response, ask others what they need from you. You will be surprised by the honesty of their response and their appreciation that you took the time to ask them.

By adopting these practices and checking with others how well they are working, you can reduce dramatically the amount of pressure that you and those people might experience.

Everyone thinks of changing the world, but no one thinks of changing himself. LEO TOLSTOY

Whatever your role is, what can you do to appreciate what can be gained from change and feel more confident to move forward into action, rather than it generating high levels of pressure?

→ **Use the support available** as there are always people around who will provide a listening ear, accept you as you are, provide positive energy and know what best to do to help you. Who is like this in your life? We often need to be more open to allowing others to support us and trust them to get it right.

→ **Maintain meaningful goals** particularly during any time you experience a sense of loss, dislocation and lack of meaning, you can alter your outlook by setting out the points that you want to get to and the outcomes you want to achieve, that would make the change successful for you. When you remind yourself about these (write them somewhere you will be accessing on a regular basis), you will be able to establish focus, make decisions and regain a balanced perspective. What would a successful outcome be from a change you are currently involved in?

→ **Accept what is inevitable** especially if commonly you attempt to control and influence areas of change that are outside of your sphere of influence: you will waste energy and create frustration. There are certain things in all of our lives that we have to accept will happen without our input. What is something you can learn to accept that inevitably will happen and change, without the need for you to invest your time and energy?

→ **Allow sufficient time** so that it will be easier not to be rushed into responding and acting quickly when you are faced with a change.

Activity

Ask yourself these questions:

When do you find yourself acting in haste, rather than stepping back, reflecting and considering a range of possibilities?

What do you need to let go of, in the short term, so you can focus on taking time to understand what is happening right now?

How can you step back from change and allow yourself the time you need to make a positive transition?

→ **Learn to ask really good questions** and you will find that there is always information, knowledge and understanding that you can seek out, to help you to feel more confident about the change you are undertaking. If you do not know what is happening or what it will mean for you, you have the right to ask the important questions. Getting in the habit of being curious to know more usually will put you in a knowledgeable and advantageous position.

What one question would you like to have answered about something changing around you?

→ **Develop a discerning approach** and you will discover that all of the people involved in a change will have different perspectives, variable levels of information, and will offer extremes of advice. Learning to listen without judging, not accepting information or views as totally true and balancing viewpoints are helpful strategies. You know best what matters to you! In what areas do you need to form your own position, not just accept what others say as valid?

I moan a lot about my ineptitude with technology and electronics. Yet over time I've learnt to make better use of new gear, at my level, without having to be an expert and know everything. Now I look forward to having conversations with people who know a lot more and tapping into the expertise available to me. By **embracing the future** you become part of its success.

What is something you fear where you have a low level of knowledge and expertise? Who can help you with this? What level of change would be okay for you?

Summary

Change creates enormous pressure for all of us but our response is the key to not allowing the experience to become stressful. The main elements that will make a difference to you and others involved in change are:

→ Recognising that different people experience change in very different ways. Therefore, if it is going to work, you and others need to be at your most tolerant and understanding, during any period of transition.

→ Focussing on what is happening now and what we want to achieve in the future, you will ease the process of shifting into a new position and state. It is easy for all of us to focus on a past golden age and over-value those times in considering our response to current change.

→ Setting an example and encouraging others to follow your lead by helping others to see what they can achieve and how they can make gains. This is because during change people look around and notice who is achieving success and gaining benefit.

The five key points to increase positivity towards change and to reduce ongoing pressure are:

→ Create a part or role for yourself and others so you appreciate the value of what you can add.

→ Get out of the detail and open your eyes to the bigger picture and the possibilities.

→ Avoid the maelstrom of the rumour mill and focus on the practical steps you can take.

→ Talk about your concerns with the right people who can then respond to them.

→ Find a reason for going to a different place. Then do something to begin to move towards achieving it.

> ## Be the change that you wish to see in the world.
>
> MAHATMA GANDHI

"Visualize yourself not falling off the wall."

Developing the support networks that you need

Chapter Seven

When a person really desires something, all the universe conspires to help that person to realise his dream. PAULO COELHO

Having read this book so far, let's get straight to the point. What is the number one way you can beat stress? In almost every situation involving pressure that I have encountered and that my clients have talked about most, what is the one answer that stands out above all others? It is the ability to build, maintain and use a support network of the right people, on a continuous basis.

As we move through pressure into stress, and ultimately distress, often we feel very alone, as if we are the only people experiencing difficulty, anxiety and concern. In reality this is usually miles away from the actual situation we are in. We all know that it is not easy to see outside, from our immediate situation, when we are in a dark forest.

Activity

Stop for a moment and really consider when you felt alone or in a dark place.

How much did you make use of the support of others to help you find warmth, care and encouragement?

Most of us do not ask for the help we need at the right time, when it will make the biggest difference. How true is this for you?

Right now, who can provide you with support?

Who will you turn to, rely on and trust when things get tough?

How much time and energy do you put into cultivating your key relationships?

This chapter is designed to encourage you to think of additional supporters, outside of the people you deal with all of the time. Some of these people will be essential for you to add to your network, as you encounter difficult times and wrestle with ongoing change.

Powering Through Pressure

Colleagues will often be more aware of the challenges you are facing than you may give them credit for. Also they will have a good understanding of your situation, as often they will be facing the same pressures as you. Are you being open with your colleagues about the things that are affecting you? If not, they will make their own guesses about what is going on. Which is better, the truth from you or informal Chinese whispers creating stories about you? To what extent do you feel comfortable about asking for their help? Remind yourself that, although they are busy and may not have noticed your concerns, they probably want to support you. Who have you helped in the past? Who in the future will be only too willing to provide support when you need it?

Your boss has a duty of care to deal with the things that are creating pressure and preventing you from doing your job. Most bosses will do the best they can to provide or arrange for additional support. However, they are not mind readers, so keeping them up to date with changes, difficulties, concerns and challenges, enables them to make better choices about what they do to affect your situation. I have heard many people complaining about the lack of support from their boss, yet these same people forget that their boss is so often immersed in their own concerns and the demands they face, that they will not be as aware as they might of your position.

Your staff are often the last people you would want to trouble or seek support from. After all, they have their own issues and difficulties. In fact, you probably want to protect them from the pressures and demands being exerted on you. A criticism I often hear voiced about bosses is that they don't keep their staff sufficiently informed and don't communicate enough about important issues. Possibly this is being said about you right now, by some of your staff. They need to know that you don't have all the answers, that you rely on their input and that you trust them. They will be more committed to you if they are consulted, and included, in dealing with and solving mutual problems.

Human Resources see it as an important part of their role to provide the best means of supporting staff to do the best they can. This also means helping managers to address and remove the issues that are creating anxiety or adding pressure. Who is the one person in HR to whom you would go when you need additional support? They also have a role in ensuring that disputes and relationship issues at work are resolved, perhaps by using mediation and other external resources, where it is necessary.

Families often are best placed just to be there and provide a listening ear when things are getting on top of us. Yet often we shield our families from work-related anxieties. Many people are willing to do almost anything when their family members need support, but are reluctant to ask those same people for their help. Remind yourself that being a true family member is a two-way obligation!

> **My friends and family are my support system. They tell me what I need to hear, not what I want to hear, and they are there for me in the good and bad times. Without them I have no idea where I would be and I know that their love for me is what's keeping my head above the water.** KELLY CLARKSON

Close friends are probably the people we have as our go-to first source of support, and as our prime resource to provide joint help to enable us to cope. Powerfully and truthfully, they restore our sense of perspective, do reality checks and give us honest feedback. In our frenetic world it's easy to lose touch, get lazy with maintaining contact and also not take the time to check out how they are. Who are the people you trust, yet haven't been in contact with for a while? Pick up the phone now!

Members of a church or spiritual group are, for many people, the source of uplifting company, providing spiritual reassurance, healing and closeness, when life is proving tough. Prayer has been shown to raise levels of confidence, ease anxiety and build positive self-esteem. Acts of compassion and empathy provide a powerful and revitalising energy when we need it most.

> **Appreciation is the highest form of prayer, for it acknowledges the presence of good**

wherever you shine the light of your thankful thoughts. ALAN COHEN

Members of groups can provide a lot of support. Research indicates that regular contact with like-thinking people involved in meditation, yoga and mindfulness sessions, proves to be an effective source of release, provides fresh social contact and considerably restores energy. They create a space for slowing down our thinking, provide ways of helping us to learn to relax, give us strategies for dealing with anxiety and physically help to restore balance. If you are a non-stop person, you will need to find a way of helping yourself to deal with all the chaotic thoughts crashing around in your brain and to have somewhere that provides slow time for physical and mental recharging. Many of the approaches and materials used by these groups are available now for use in the home or can work as a social energy activator, when used with friends. Consider the power, fun and rejuvenating effect of technology such as Wii.

Professional bodies and business networks reinforce the messages that we need to hear when we are experiencing pressure: that we are not the only ones facing difficult situations. It is reassuring and confidence boosting to be able to learn from others who are in similar situations, and who have found ways of dealing with the pressures they encountered. Having a strong base of knowledge that is up to date, also gives us a great lift in confidence when we are under pressure to deal with business demands. Which group could provide a means for you to meet with like-thinking people? The right groups are, for many, the only 'safe' place where issues are able to be discussed, without the anxiety about the consequences of confiding in co-workers in your own organisation. Have you thought about forming your own group with some of the people that you respect and trust?

GPs or nursing staff are an essential first port of call when you are experiencing the physical signs of growing pressure. Given that over 40 per cent of GP ailments now have a link to some form of stress, GPs are used to at least pointing you in the right direction, and supporting your short-term needs through medication, where it is appropriately diagnosed. Many medical staff now are trained additionally in a wide range of complementary therapies, or an integrated support team is available within practices. You do not have to continue to put up with aches and pains, when relevant expertise is readily available.

Occupational Health staff provide a great first checkpoint, when all sorts of pressures are beginning to have an effect on employee health. They are often in the advantageous position of knowing the specific pressures that exist within a particular organisation. Their familiarity with company health and well-being policies means that they are useful generators of a range of possible available options and health schemes.

Employee Assistance Programmes have proved to be one of the most powerfully effective sources of professional support. Counselling and other services are offered as part of a company-supported Employee Assistance Programme (EAP). Many people see this as a last resort, but forget that the help they provide is a non-judgemental, highly professional and confidential service, which, if used early in the pressure process, can prevent stress. Many schemes include legal, financial, relationship and personal consultation, which helps clients to understand the many options and achieve a clear sense of direction and purpose. This can be invaluable in preventing stress, and is relevant for everyone! Where people are on long-term absence due to health issues, ongoing counselling can provide the strongest help to managers and staff to help to put in place the means for sustaining recovery. Specialist services, such as trauma and critical incident support, can prove a life saver when individuals and groups are caught up in the pressures generated by serious incidents, such as robberies, deaths and accidents at work.

Other counselling or psychotherapy helps when people are referred for ongoing, face-to-face counselling support, providing an essential lifeline, particularly for people who are affected by depression and other mental health issues. The development and use of practical, solution-centred psychotherapies, such as cognitive behaviour therapy, generally have made seeking this form of help a much more acceptable and respected choice. There is now much less stigma attached to working with a therapist.

Mental health groups, like MIND, provide specific help to anyone who is experiencing thinking and 'state of mind' issues. This can range from working with a loss of confidence and reduced self-esteem, to aiding recovery during clinical depression. Given that one in four of us will experience some form of mental health issue at some point in our lives, groups and practitioners in this arena provide a critical service in getting to the heart of issues and encouraging people to think about their pressure condition in different ways.

Outplacement is a support usually available for those experiencing redundancy or job loss. When this change occurs, it is not easy for those affected to even consider, let alone develop, a range of options. Best use is made often when people are struggling to remain balanced in their decision making and battling with the emotions that are triggered. Receiving unbiased support in this arena will help to work through the apparent chaos, uncertainty and disorder. In that way it is easier to stay focussed, and remain as positive as possible.

With greater knowledge of the support available to most people, it is easier to seek out the most appropriate help and inform others so they can make the best choices when they need help.

You are not on your own; you are part of a team!

My research has also identified that many people do not make use of or create opportunities for others, given the potential support that is available within work teams. We have identified a set of team practices that are critical to building individual and group resilience. Where this team strength and toughness exists there is a strong correlation to reduced levels of pressure and higher levels of performance under difficult conditions.

Activity

Consider the elements in building team resilience and ask yourself:

How do I and my teams perform on building and continuing to use each of these elements?

Elements essential to building team resilience

1 What is your **support** network like?

2 How easy is it to **ask for** or **offer help**?

3 What level of **ongoing feedback** do you give and receive?

4 What **goals** are you and others working towards?

▶

---

5 To what extent are **issues** discussed openly?

6 What do you share as group **values**?

7 How often do you **recognise and celebrate success**?

8 Is it okay to have **fun**?

9 How much **shared learning** occurs?

10 What **opportunities** do you create for each other?

Now, identify which of these you could make more of an effort to promote and take the initiative to develop within the team.

1 Building a powerful network ideally means building a diverse group of people close around you. Where you have this, you will be able to learn from each other's approach, draw on varied experience and provide different types of help.

2 Many people feel as if they should not ask for help and that they must continue to deal with difficulties themselves. This is perceived often as 'toughing it out'.

3 Regularly checking how others are and being alert to changes in others' temperament and behaviour will enable your entire group to know when to step in.

4 Only by giving and receiving feedback will individuals know what is working and what is not. Where this is not an accepted process, group members are left feeling anxious and uncertain, resulting in more hesitant behaviour. Feedback provides the impetus for group members to recognise the need to change, in order to reduce pressure.

5 Having shared goals that others have been involved in developing, and are committed to, will enable everyone to stay focussed and to concentrate on what is important. This is crucial when situations change or become more complex and difficult.

6 The pressure in groups is increased often when issues, concerns and problems are not discussed. Therefore, it is essential that situations that may create tension and anxiety are able to be raised

in a non-blaming way. Where this openness exists, groups focus on solving problems, rather than ignoring them or hoping they will go away.

7   When individuals operate outside of what they believe matters, then it is difficult to get the energy and commitment of group members to take risks and do things in different ways. Our values consciously need to drive the desired group behaviours, as issues are dealt with and decisions made. Based on clear values, these actions will provide reassurance and build trust. Where this happens, group members will recognise where situations and behaviour are out of kilter and are generating unnecessary pressure. Members can remind each other what they have agreed is acceptable behaviour.

8   Under pressure most individuals need more positive recognition and an environment where people focus on what is working, how to achieve success and recognising progress made. This state will help to maintain the morale and motivation that is crucial during periods of change. It is widely recognised that when times are difficult we need three times as many positives, in order for us to accept them as valid. Confidence levels and positive self-esteem will be strongly affected by negativity, emphasis on failure, unsolved problems and perceived lack of progress.

9   Effectively resilient groups recognise the need to play regularly as well as work hard. I notice immediately within work environments those that are fun places to be in. Some areas I encounter appear to have an atmosphere that reminds me of what I have read of Dickensian workhouses. One powerful way of reducing pressure levels is to have regular opportunities that lighten the atmosphere, allow people to joke (even if it is at the expense of the boss) and deemed where laughter moments are encouraged, whenever it is deemed appropriate.

10   Part of the pressure we all experience comes from a sense that we may not have the knowledge, skills and experience to cope with changes and deal with difficult situations. One answer is to provide continuously the means for group members to share information, pass on knowledge and coach each other in new skills development. Where this is reinforced by recognition from

management, a rich resource evolves that, in times of difficulty, can be mined.

11 When we become focussed on current difficulties and are anxious about the future, it is not easy to look forward with optimism and enthusiasm. Groups can increase the levels of positive thinking, approaches and behaviour, by concentrating on working through challenges together, and creating additional opportunities to learn from each other.

Building support doesn't just happen, you have to work at it!

Like many of the other skills I have referred to throughout this book, developing your best support network is something to which you need to dedicate time and continue to put effort into evolving. An up-to-date set of positive relationships provides an accessible resource. We have looked at a diverse range of successful networkers and deduced some of the principles that differentiate them as having a ready-made source of support.

Activity

How effective are you at creating and sustaining a support network?

Answer the following questions:

Do you embrace the philosophy of 'what I give = what I gain?'
People who learn to give easily often will appreciate what can be gained through their actions and others' responses. All of us will have experienced times when we moved forward by investing energy into others, particularly when we discovered fresh ways of doing things. At that time, we took pleasure in seeing their success and how they were recognised for their achievements, influenced by our efforts. They often provided different perspectives, views and ideas for us to make use of in the future.

Do you approach your networks and contacts in a disciplined, rigorous way?

For any meeting or business occasion, particularly those that are deemed important, consider as part of your planning how this 'event' will provide an opportunity for you to strengthen your relationships. Consider who is going to be at a future event that you have not seen for some time. What would you like to know from them? What would you like to let them know about you? When was the last time that you came back from an event and recorded useful notes about others who attended?

Do you plan your networking at least every six months?

How do you ensure that you stay in touch?

It is helpful to sit down on a regular basis to evaluate your current key relationships and identify where your network could be strengthened. Who is currently missing from your regular network? When this practice becomes a regular habit, then you will be able to automatically include networking activities more easily as integral to your weekly and monthly plans, allocating the resources you need.

Do you let others know what you are doing?

Keeping on the radar of the people who really matter to you is an essential business skill. You can do this by remembering important occasions, following up on meetings, sending updates or newsletters, asking for information, and meeting socially around birthdays or Christmas. Now we also have the advantage of being able to regularly update using internet networking sites, such as LinkedIn.

Do you have role models to which you refer?

Do you use a coach or a mentor?

It can be very lonely at work and it is not easy to open up, particularly when things are tough or you are experiencing big changes. Having a confidante, a reflector of your thinking, a sharer of experience and an empathetic listener is essential when pressure builds up. Role models also provide inspiration and the impetus to improve or change the way we think and do things. Who do you know, who is a successful role model? What can you learn from them? What would you gain from having a coach or mentor?

▶

Have you become a great storyteller and balanced listener?
Some of the most powerful lessons we learn in dealing with difficulty come about as a result of us sharing experiences and then being responsive to the reactions and changes these opportunities trigger. Learning to articulate with energy will enable you to get others' attention, interest and support. Stories are a powerful source of influence that often are undervalued and underused. Consider a great storyteller you know and what you have learnt from them. What stories do you have that others would be interested in?

Do you have a database of resources to help yourself and others identify the best source of support?
You are probably a greater store of knowledge, contacts and links to resources than you give yourself credit for. At this point, you probably hold some of the answers to others' dilemmas and issues. The more you share willingly and are curious, the greater the resource pool that is available to everyone.

World makers, social network makers, ask one question first: 'How can I do it?'

ZADIE SMITH

How open are you to new people and new thinking?
We get very used to doing things in the same way with the same people, who often are similar in thinking and behaviour to ourselves. When the pressure is on, you need fresh insights, different approaches and alternative behaviours. Instead of surrounding yourself with clones because it is easy, think about putting yourself in more situations where your current approach and thinking is challenged.

Do you take sufficient time to make building relationships a critical part of your life?
As we move into facing up to challenges often we look only for processes, systems, tools and technology as the way of improving the situation or solving problems. They are part of the answer but, in most of the difficult situations you will face, it is what you do with others that will make the biggest difference. How much of your energy and time do you put into

rigorously cultivating new relationships? What would you have to do to demonstrate that you value your time with others? What do you need from others that would make a difference to you?

Do you regularly share best practice?
Here is a new habit that could change your way of dealing with difficulties. Each time you, and your colleagues, discover new thinking, different practices or achieve a success, set up an agreement that the important information is passed on within your work group. So much of the pressure that comes from repetitive effort, lost time and issues about responsibility can be prevented by the clear communication of learning within groups and businesses. What is something you have learnt this week? Who would gain by being aware of this? Keep a learning diary, useful as a bonus when you are looking to change roles.

Do you test out approaches, experiment with others and co-coach? Colleagues, friends and other peers can provide a diverse source of ideas, can challenge your thinking without being a threat, and can provide inspiration through their example. Are you missing out on opportunities to sit down with others and work things through for mutual benefit? Who are some of your team-mates or partners that you are not making use of? Who may be facing similar issues and challenges and what are they doing?

If you have answered more than five of these questions with 'no', then you cannot be sure that you will have the strength of network needed to support you the next time you are under pressure and want to prevent the onset of stress, with its debilitating chronic patterns. For a long time I was too lazy to put in the effort needed to build my network. Now it is what keeps me afloat personally and my business buoyant.

Summary

Networking and building a strong support group around you is not a 'nice to-do' activity, it is an essential ongoing business and personal skill. To have the right people around us, on each other's radar and maintaining contact is ultra-important. This needs to be supported by an attitude and willingness to engage in give and take, and to foster a strong sense through having alert antennae, so that you can look out for others who need your help.

The four key points for maximising your support will be:

→ Regularly reviewing who you have the right level of contact and quality of relationship with on your key relationship map.

→ When pressure is building up, looking for the best people to help you, before you move into a stressed state.

→ Knowing what resources are available to help you and others get the most appropriate help at the time that it is needed.

→ Being willing to ask for support and seeking others out when you are anxious or uncertain. I have learnt that I do not have to 'tough it out'. It is enormously reassuring knowing that I can trust others to provide the support when I ask. But they can do that only if I let them know what is going on.

If you are serious about developing the best support network, I recommend that you approach someone in the next few days to check out how they are, and to update them on what you are doing and the challenges you are facing. They will value it! You might also learn something that produces a great result in dealing with those challenges, or provides an opportunity that you were completely unaware of.

> **Was it you or I who stumbled first? It does not matter. The one of us who finds the strength to get up first, must help the other.** VERA NAZARIAN

Building your personal resilience; the ultimate antidote to stress

Chapter Eight

Sometimes you win and sometimes you learn.

JOHN MAXWELL

As my work on pressure and stress has evolved, there is one outstanding part that has assumed growing importance for me and, more importantly, many of my clients. This is the capability to build up, and make use of, all the core elements that encompass personal resilience. I have observed that, where there are low levels of resilience, the route from experiencing challenge to suffering from distress, is dramatically shortened. The opposite learning is just as evident. With highly developed levels of resilience, you can counter and manage the pressure, dramatically reducing the risk of the onset and development of stress.

If we concentrate on developing all of the resilience factors, inevitably we will take better care of ourselves, thus ensuring that we have the energy and health to sustain our efforts at reducing the issues and sources of our difficulties. This is in contrast to what I observe often happens, a preoccupation with the things that are happening and neglecting our health state.

Personal case study

I worked with Steve, an engineer, when he was going through a particularly difficult period of his life. He had, personally, been taking on more and more work during the previous three months, at a time when there were big changes within his work team. He was becoming disheartened, which was further draining his available energy. This was also having an effect on his close personal relationships. Just when he was starting to get on top of his workload, largely by working long hours, his mother became seriously ill. He was expected to be the pillar of support within his family.

Steve was open to our discussions about changing some things that would see him through the next three months and to find ways of raising his energy levels to meet the increased demands. He was worried that, if he didn't make some clear decisions and take immediate action, he could sink into depression. This was a real concern, as serious mental health issues were commonplace within his family.

Most importantly, he realised that he needed to draw on several elements of his resilience if he was going to really get out of the mire. First, having a strong value about honesty, he decided he needed to be straight with his manager and colleagues about what work was realistic and possible, given all that was happening. This focus allowed him to prioritise better and feel confident about negotiating the work he was asked to take on.

Second, he realised that he needed to use his close network to ask about and get some professional health support. In fact, as he talked with colleagues and friends, he realised how common his predicament was and this allowed him to be more open with them about what he needed at this time.

Third, he decided to get back into exercise by starting to play badminton again, with his partner, at least twice a week. This recharged his batteries and allowed them to spend committed time doing something they both enjoyed, together. He was a good player and his renewed success on the court and his improved relationship dramatically raised his overall confidence and self-esteem.

These were all strengths that Steve had available to draw upon as potential resources but, like many of us, he failed to appreciate and value how important they were in staying on top of things and feeling that he had control.

So, what is resilience?

We define resilience as our ability to deal with, manage and productively experience continuous change, especially in cumulatively difficult situations, or during periods when our confidence and self-esteem may have been knocked. It is during these times that we notice we need to draw on those extra resources that we hope we have available, but often take for granted. It takes years of work for us to build up a full set of resilience factors and we need to strengthen and add to our repertoire continuously. This then will enable us to pick ourselves up, keep going and push through into a stronger position and state, when the pressure is really on. Most of us will think of it as 'toughing it out', 'seeing it through' or 'getting back on our feet'.

In the workplace, resilience is now one of the essential competencies, particularly given the constant change, fast pace, demands to achieve more and greater expectations that most people have to deal with.

To assess your current levels of resilience, consider these statements:

	True	Partly True	Untrue
I am clear about my job purpose, goals and expectations			
I make use of my values when I make decisions			
I use the support from people in my network			
I develop my network continuously			
I am determined to see activities through to completion			
I follow up to ensure things happen			
I am flexible when I need to do things differently			
I am realistic about what can be achieved			
I ensure that I get the right blend of work and other activity			
I regularly seek out different ways of learning			
I know what my strengths are and play to these			
I seek feedback from others and use it			

Understanding your scoring

The items you have scored as true are likely to be the areas that you rely on when you need to be resilient. They have provided the means for you to manage difficulty, change and any shift in confidence. They are your default setting. Are you maximising them?

The items that you have scored as partly true, you probably use selectively in certain situations to help you get through, make the final push or select when other areas of resilience have not worked. How can you use these more often and in different situations?

The items you have scored as untrue are those areas of resilience you do not draw on. They are likely to be helpful when all else has failed. How can you start to value and develop these? In what situations will they prove valuable?

What are your immediate observations having completed this short questionnaire?

The six core elements of resilience

The short form of my full questionnaire, 'the personal resilience index', below, will have given you some clues about which areas of your resilience you can work on and develop. These are summarised within six core categories. For each of these I recommend you read the description, decide what you want to improve, and complete the relevant questions and activities listed. Then you will be clearer about what you need to be focussing on, can refer back to and know that you can draw upon, when you find yourself in situations that really stretch you.

The six core elements of resilience

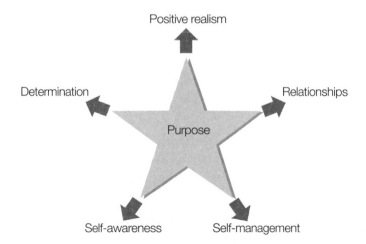

Positive realism

Determination

Relationships

Purpose

Self-awareness

Self-management

1 Sense of purpose

This is the core component of the six and the foundation for all of the others. Not everyone is clear about their purpose and it is frequently something that you will need to redefine as you move through different stages of your life. It is also worth you revisiting at regular intervals within your job. The stronger your sense of purpose, the better equipped you are to handle challenges and setbacks and to recover from them. When you encounter difficulties, having clarity of purpose will enable you to stay focussed and know what you most need to put your energy into. At any point you can refer back to those important things that you are actually there to do and that are the true purpose of your role. It is also helpful to remind yourself how your work fits within the bigger picture of the objectives agreed by your function, department or specialism.

You will be able to identify when you lack purpose because you will appear aimless, unfocussed, and will be drawn into unimportant detail and your values will be called into question.

Activity

Developing your purpose activity plan

Take some time to write down the actual purpose of your job.

My job is there to ...

What directions do you want to take in your life and work?

How does your job fit with others? Ask some key people for their perception.

What are your specific goals for this year, month and week?

Do you understand the purpose of all the activities you engage in? If not, seek clarification.

Identify three activities you do that do not fit with your purpose and goals.

Identify what you could be doing that is not part of your current remit.

What is an ambition you have for your current role?

How are you using your values in your work right now?

Which values could you make more use of and rely on to make decisions when you experience difficulties?

2 Positive realism

> **Positive thinking is great, but I am more of a positive realist. I believe anything can happen, but it often doesn't!** KELLI JAE BAELI

This component is usually something of a balancing act, between being able to think positively and aim high concerning situations and events, whilst being realistic about what pragmatically can be achieved. It is not about some naive false optimism! First we need to be able to generate positive thoughts and feelings about situations. Do you have the ability to take reality checks, to reduce the chance of creating unreasonable expectations and subsequent disappointment, for yourself and others?

Second, it is useful in difficult situations or when you face big dilemmas to use a balance sheet approach. Ask yourself what will help and what you know will not work. Check with others as to what they think will achieve the best results and what will limit what can be done.

Your positive realism will be low when you find yourself stretched to the limit by over-demanding situations and you feel negative about what can be achieved. You can also notice yourself setting unrealistic expectations that may be disempowering others as well as yourself. Do you hear, 'This is impossible' or 'It cannot be done.'?

Activity

Developing your positive realism activity plan:

Identify three things that are currently working well for you.

What is it about certain difficult situations that can elicit negative responses from you?

When you are successful, what do you do to remain positive?

Identify three things you feel optimistic about.

When do you have unrealistic expectations about yourself and/or others?

What is the effect of this?

Take a difficult situation you are facing. Sort the facts from your 'biased'

▶

---

perception of what is occurring. Ask someone else for their observations about the situation.

What negativity do you pick up from others?

Who can provide a more positive outlook?

How will you spend more time with them?

How do you keep yourself grounded about what is really possible and achievable? Consider who you know who is very good at this balancing act.

What do they do differently?

3 Quality relationships

People matter to all of us, whatever we are doing, so building challenging, supportive and caring relationships is essential. Your interpersonal communication and skills can be the most important element affecting your ability to remain resilient. It will dictate whether you have the flexibility to consider and use a range of ways of dealing with difficult situations or getting through tough times.

It is also powerful to be able to offer appropriate support to others and to ask for help when you need to. Consider what you do at times to stop yourself from seeking out others when you most need help.

Achieving a balance of challenge and support will determine whether you can get the best from the relationships that matter under pressure. You will be able to judge the quality of your relationships by the levels of honesty, openness, clarity of communication and truth-telling that you experience. When we are in trouble we need others to be straight with us and we also need to level with them. You will need to create the atmosphere amongst your contacts that supports this sincerity, frankness and authenticity. That is why it is so important to be yourself throughout the different areas of your life, not play the role that you and others may think is appropriate.

Developing your quality relationship activity plan

Consider your current support network to identify ways it could be strengthened.

Who are you not using and what can they offer?

Who would be a real asset when you are under pressure to have in your close network?

Set up a co-coaching arrangement with a close friend or work colleague. Agree to meet when either of you are feeling really stretched or are struggling with something important.

Who may be in difficulty, to whom you could give support?

Remind yourself what you will do to ensure you are aware when others need your help and support.

4 Developing determination yet remaining open-minded and flexible

At its core this aspect of resilience is all about seeing things through. When you are faced with challenges, you deal with them by using a 'can do' approach, becoming more proactive and knowing when it is time to take action. Alongside these characteristics, consider how well you finish off or complete tasks, your willingness to be open to different ideas and ensure that you follow up on things that you have started.

This type of resilience means that you know you are able to keep going in the face of adversity or when you encounter resistance, rather than give up. You can be adaptable and open-minded to others', thinking or fresh ideas. In this way you are able to provide yourself with a greater range of choices for dealing with new or very different situations.

Your levels are low if you find yourself with many unfinished tasks, relationships that are 'all over the place', losing the will to go on, operating in reactive ways and becoming more inactive. You will notice that obstacles and issues dominate your thinking, rather than solutions, making progress and resolution.

Developing your determination yet open-minded activity plan

What is one thing that is unfinished and generating pressure for you and others?

What will you and others need to do to move forward?

Look around your workplace and home to identify four things that need work, or that you want to complete. Allocate a specific time to get these things done.

Put in place a review/feedback process with all the important tasks you are undertaking.

Take a decision you need to make and identify (with others' support if necessary) four different alternatives.

Where does 'analysis paralysis' get in the way of you and others moving forward? Take one situation. Stop the analysis and thinking. Make a decision. Now move into action.

Where are you being inflexible? Decide on one area and decide how you can loosen your position to enable you to effectively negotiate a solution.

5 Self-awareness

The component of self-awareness applies to the ways that you use your knowledge, the understanding of your inner self, and how you think, feel and react. The greater your clarity in these elements, the more you will be in control of your situation. Your responses will then come from being aware of the unproductive or productive patterns you have in the way you think about, or respond to, different situations and challenges.

Resilient people are able to identify what specifically contributes to their success when they are dealing with challenges and issues. Then they can learn from their conclusions and realisations and move on in their lives. Seeking out the views of others also provides a balanced view of what you are doing, the impact you are having and what is working.

Success also comes from recognising what is within your control and influence. Fighting battles and struggling with challenges that you cannot control or influence only produces greater anxiety and frustration.

You will recognise low levels of self-awareness when you repeat the same mistakes, fail to spot when approaches are not working, realise your perspectives on relationships are very different to others, and find yourself stuck at similar points in a project or activity.

6 Self-management and self-reliance

The final component of self-management examines how well you use your skills and work in the right ways to maximise available resources. This includes how effectively you manage your time and a common strength is very visible when we ensure that we take on only what we can handle realistically and know we can deliver. Over-commitment and potential under-delivery generates high levels of pressure for so many people.

Resilience also will come from being mindful to make sure that you have the right blend of all of the important aspects or your work and life. To achieve this, you will check that you take responsibility for yourself and your actions. This dramatically contrasts with people who struggle to make their mark because they will not accept responsibility and often will hold others accountable for everything that happens. Taking responsibility requires a lot of vitality and for this you need to look after yourself and have a lifestyle that maintains your energy.

Strangely, a contrasting part of this component is the ability to stand alone, work and focus by yourself and provide your own structure and plans when required to take on challenges.

People with low levels of self-management are spotted very easily. They appear constantly frantic, short-change themselves and others in terms of meeting needs, and abuse their own time. Consequently, others feel under-valued as a resource in their lives. The unmanaged lifestyle is chaotic and those consumed by it generally unhealthy and uncaring about their physical, emotional and mental well-being. If this sounds harsh, look around you.

Activity

Your self-management activity plans

In what areas are you not taking care of yourself? Produce a plan for changing this situation.

Identify the most important areas in your life and work. Produce a pie chart of the right blend for you over the next three months.

What is one thing in your life that is stealing your time? Decide how you will stop it.

How are you using effectively the resources at your disposal?

What one resource could you make better use of, to support you during difficult times?

Where are you over-committing? What will you need to give up or let go of?

What do you do that gives you energy and recharges your batteries? How will you ensure that you do enough of these activities and habits, to see you through the next six months?

The time that we need our depth of resilience most is when we are attempting to lead a normal life, whilst facing major life challenges, such as deaths of those close to us, break up of important relationships, major financial issues, big role changes and loss of work.

How can your resilience work to get you through difficult periods?

Clarity of values and focussing on what you can achieve.

At a time when our whole world can feel as if it has been put into a spin, we need to be able to make some decisions and take appropriate actions. To do this, we need to remind ourselves about the things in our life at that point, which are most important to us. This may mean taking time out to spend with others who share our situation, know us well or who have a clear understanding of what we are going through. We can then decide on a small number of goals that will help us to move forward. Translating these into small steps can provide a reinforcing sense of progress and optimism.

Personal case study

Derek had been made redundant and, having worked hard to build his own business, he faced bankruptcy after losing two major clients. They had transferred to using cheaper, non-UK suppliers. Unsurprisingly, by experiencing a second major business setback within a short space of time, considerable emotional strain was created and he experienced a major loss of confidence in his decision making.

In our work together, he identified the three values he most adhered to in his business life: honesty and truth-telling, support of his colleagues and openness of communication. From this, he decided that he would talk to as many people as possible in order to have a better chance of finding ways out of his predicament. This included talking to financial institutions, professional bodies and local business support groups.

His rediscovered openness, as he sought out fresh ideas, as well as financial and other job options, raised his spirits. It also generated several opportunities and prompted a surprising offer of collaboration. This, ultimately, led to a new business plan that eased his current position and established the ongoing support he so badly needed.

Derek's example also illustrates the importance of continuously building and using the people within your network. Often it is only when we are in difficulty that we take advantage of consulting or involving those who can provide the knowledge, skills and information we do not have personally accessible. If we get in the habit of regular exchange, then we have a ready store for when the going gets tough.

The ability to use an approach based on **positive realism** will come about only if we adopt a process of 'continuous lessons learnt'. Throughout projects and major activity streams, we need to learn to assess regularly and negotiate over what is possible and realistic. Otherwise our expectations can far exceed our ability to deliver. If we add a process that continuously reinforces what is working, then we are more capable of conducting reality checks and maintaining a positive construct. This is invaluable when things appear negative and it is so easy for us all to become 'depressed'.

This approach will often overlap with the resilience mode of **flexible determination**.

Personal case study

Christine found herself in a 'disastrous, terrible scenario', following a serious accident involving her sister. This resulted in her sibling needing full-time care, at a time when she was experiencing her own incapacitating health issues. She was plunged suddenly into despair about how they would manage and could think about only what was happening now in pessimistic terms.

This was a person who had grown up successfully, despite living in a 'tough environment', had gone on to over-achieve academically against all expectations, and had worked to gain promotion into senior roles. What she had not learnt to do, as she dramatically overcame obstacles, was to acknowledge this determination to succeed and to internally register her overriding sense of 'can do'. These strengths proved what she could achieve, far above what might be possible for many others.

As we worked through her life story and her many achievements, she had one of those rare enlightening moments. She realised finally how much character she had drawn on internally to overcome whatever had been thrown at her.

With some panache she launched into a new-found, positively achieving mode and quickly set up the means to adapt and flex her role, strengthen her physical energy reserves and obtain the family care needed.

The capacity to establish strong self-confidence and high self-esteem, can come about through seeking out, receiving and acting upon feedback. What this develops is the sense of learning from everything we do, and allowing ourselves to recognise and celebrate success. When a tough event like a relationship break-up occurs, this capacity will enable us to hold onto the perception that we are 'okay as a person' and have the balance needed to move forward into other relationships with strengthened resolve.

Our **self-management** resilience skills will, if grown through learning to appreciate resources early in our life, provide the blend of approaches needed to establish a sense of being back in control. This is true particularly when demands crowd in and others' expectations threaten to exceed our capacity to deliver. Health issues often appear to be overwhelming, because our understanding is driven more by fear of the unknown, than knowledge of what is available and possible.

I found that at the worst point of a serious heart-related illness, what helped most was the capacity always to seek to understand and know more. I could then make **my** decisions about treatment, based on a number of options. Knowing where I was in my recovery process through regular progress checks and self monitoring, encouraged me to adhere more rigorously to the treatment regimes. Without learning as I went, asking the right questions and always discussing options, I would have struggled to know how best to build and sustain my strength, and stay responsibly in control of my situation.

Summary

Already you have evolved strong elements of resilience based on developing a clear purpose, your capability to build and use relationships, your determination to succeed, your capacity to remain positively optimistic, your skill and knowledge to generate options and your inner confidence that you have used to sustain progress despite setbacks.

There are several factors that will help you to tap into and make use of these elements of resilience, when you are under pressure:

→ Learning as much from success and what you get right, as from the things that don't work. Adopt a balance sheet mentality in all difficult situations.

→ Crediting yourself with and acknowledging what you have done and learnt already throughout your life. Under pressure, ask yourself, 'What do I know?' and 'What can I do?'

→ Identifying and drawing on all the resources you have available, when you need them. When things get tough, look about you and spy those who will make a positive difference batting for your team.

→ Reminding yourself that you are at the same time a potentially vulnerable, yet immensely strong human who has, in many ways, survived and flourished successfully. When you are in doubt or anxious, ask yourself, 'What have I done before?'

Ultimately, resilience is of value only if you make use of all the internal and external resources you have available to take actions that will help you and others to move forward, stay strong and remain positively engaged.

> **Resilience is not a commodity you are born with, waiting silently on tap. It is self-manufactured painstakingly over time by working through your problems and never giving up, even in the face of difficulty or failure.** LORII MYERS, *NO EXCUSES; THE FIT MIND-FIT BODY STRATEGY BOOK*

Powering Through Pressure

Reducing your pressure throughout the year

Chapter Nine

This chapter is designed so that you can consider the theme associated with each month and take actions to reduce stress throughout the year triggered by the thoughts I have included.

Month	Theme	Your actions
January	Personal and team planning	
February	Looking out for the people who really matter	
March	Financial housekeeping	
April	Starting afresh and making the most of newness	
May	Supporting others through pressured time	
June	Making the most of events and occasions	
July	Seizing our opportunities and allaying fears	
August	Actually enjoying holidays and rejuvenation	
September	Moving on, letting go	
October	Acting now to pre-empt SAD	
November	Making the most of our life and work roles	
December	Keeping sane and well throughout the Christmas period	

January

> We spend January walking through our lives, room by room, drawing up a list of work to be done, cracks to be patched. Maybe this year, to balance the list, we ought to walk through the rooms of our lives ... not looking for flaws, but for potential. ELLEN GOODMAN

January is the month that should be the start of new and great things, but for many people is the 'dark' month. Long nights, days of snow and continuous cold combine with a strong sense of anti-climax to leave people feeling down. We even have 'Blue Monday' when there are more calls made to help lines than on any other day in the year. Credit card summaries show how much many of us have overspent during the festive period. Hospitals are bursting at the seams. All around us on public transport fellow travellers cough, sneeze and wheeze. Is it any wonder that we can't wait to finish the month? Do the Chinese have it right by starting their new year in February?

So what do we do to survive?

Start the year by holding over some Christmas treats that will re-energise you, and share these occasions with your favourite people.

Pamper days, afternoon teas, favourite walks and theatre experiences are all offered at special rates at this time of year.

It is also time to ask others to do things to meet your needs. Many of you will have 'slaved' away over the Christmas period, so it is time for others to step up and do things to take care of the needs you have suppressed in caring for others.

Rather than making New Year resolutions, wait until the month has started to unfold and then take some brief timeout to develop a personal and team plan for the year. Involve other key people in identifying the key things that jointly you want to achieve and do from each of the following six areas. Our ritual incentive is to carry out the 'planning meeting' over a nice meal and with some very decent wine.

What will you do this year within these areas of your life?

→ **Holidays and travel plans** What sort of holidays would you love to have? What mix of timeout do you want? What is your budget? What is possible? What normally would you not consider yet could provide a brilliant experience? When are the best times when you most need to take a break? It's totally okay to include allocating time at home to do the stuff you don't get around to doing during the rest of the year.

→ **Home improvements or work (or moves)** What needs doing? What is bugging you that you want to change? What will add value or brighten your environment? What energy-related changes are being offered by the Government or utility schemes? What can you do now to your garden that will light up your spring and summer?

→ **Family, relationship and friend building** Who do you want to spend more time with? What opportunities are there to get together? Who do you want in your key relationship network? What do you want to do together to enrich and value your personal time?

→ **Health and fitness gains** What changes will you make to your eating, activity and health regimes? What incentives are there to make these changes? For which occasions do you want to look and feel better? What events will provide the impetus to put in exercise hours? What social opportunities or hobbies can you combine with exercise?

→ **Work and personal learning** What do you want to learn to do this year? What skills can you develop and take further? What is on offer to provide different experiences and learning? What have you always wanted to learn to do?

→ **Financial** How clear are you about your financial position? What do you have available to invest? How do you want to use any spare cash? How could you reduce spending? What are the best ways of saving or investing for you?

Here are some steps that you can take to increase your chances of succeeding in doing more of the things that will energise your life and reduce pressure.

→ Play about with, and be open to, a whole range of possibilities. At this point you are identifying only hopes, ambitions and desires. Allow your curiosity to rule so that you know what is out there.

→ Decide what the **one** most important action is for you in each area.

→ Set specific outcomes and targets. Done in this way, you can see the whole year unfolding in positive and actionable ways, and you can plan more easily.

→ Keep your goals in a special place, such as a really nice book that you know you will want to dip back into. If you plan electronically, set up an easily accessible online file, or a regular reminder system.

→ At the end of each month, transfer key information onto the calendars that you refer to weekly. The more hopes and desires you have in front of you, the more likely you are to take action. Regularly remind each other what you said you would do.

→ Be prepared to flex your intentions as you go. All our circumstances change and new opportunities will suggest actions that become higher priorities.

→ Use your goals as rewards for the hard work you inevitably will put in throughout the year.

And, if you want to be really serious about what to do in the coming year, take note of what your astrologer is saying!

If you don't know where you are going, you'll end up someplace else. YOGI BERRA

February

> **May this time be filled with love, understanding and contentment as you journey through life with those you hold dear.** DARLY HENERSON

February is the month that many people just want to get through and move on from. Fighting our way through snow, cold and wet, hastily passing the dark shadows that are our neighbours, is all part of our struggle to survive the final ravages of winter. Many of us look at our pale reflections in the mirror and wonder in consternation what we can do to look and feel better.

It is easy to become self-critical, spend our days lazing indoors and losing contact with others. What we miss are the beginnings of new life that are bursting through frozen ground, so small yet so beautiful. So, if you do nothing else during this month, get wrapped up and walk out there on those rare, fine and crisp days, and spy out every snowdrop and crocus you can discover. It will be uplifting.

February can also highlight how many people feel alone, abandoned, ignored and isolated. This at a time when we have the opportunity to celebrate Valentine's Day properly, the biggest festival of love, care and adoration of other people that we have. What this can become for many of us is the opportunity to look outside ourselves and remember the people who really matter to us.

This period can, therefore, represent the ideal time of rebuilding, reconnecting and reaffirming our care for others.

Take some time out right now to consider who you want in your life, which relationships you want to build and who you want to recognise for what they bring to your life. It is a great time to examine consciously your network and make clear decisions about the people who will, on a reciprocal basis, provide the sustainable links you will need and rely on. Consider who will energise you when your batteries are running down. Who can you call up when you are feeling low? Who can you celebrate with, when you achieve and have successes during the year?

Key relationship map

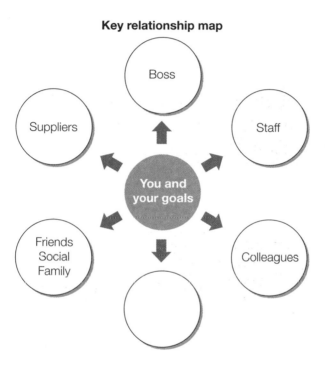

Twice a year I draw up my key relationship map, a fancy name for reminding myself who I need in my life and want to put energy into to provide the mutual support that will help me to achieve joint goals and feel valued. Then I use the following activity to ensure I have the right people on my radar and that I appear on theirs.

1 Place people in each category according to how much time and energy you currently put into the relationship.

2 Rate the current quality of that relationship and what words you would use to describe how you are with each other, e.g. cool, close, distant, difficult, fun, casual, argumentative, etc.

3 Identify the importance of that person in influencing what you do (High 5, Low 1).

4 Where do I want to change the nature of the relationship?

Then I ask these questions:

Who have I not seen for some time that I want to refresh my relationship with?

Who would value a call from me?

Who have I met this year whom I want to further develop a relationship with?

Who might need my support right now?

Who will support me when I need it? Who can I ask for help?

Interestingly, the more energy we put into supporting and helping others, the more we reduce our anxieties and self-concerns. It's a bit like switching off our internal pressure system and turning on our external caring system.

Go and see someone now!

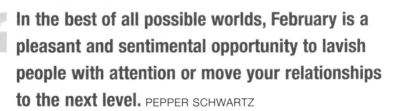

In the best of all possible worlds, February is a pleasant and sentimental opportunity to lavish people with attention or move your relationships to the next level. PEPPER SCHWARTZ

March

March is one of the most powerfully influential months in so many ways. We associate this time as bursting with new life and hope, freshness and vital energy. It is the great restorer, suggesting promise, positive hope and optimism about what is to come. Given this awakening, we need to savour this period with all our senses and ensure we build in as many opportunities as possible, to fill our energy tanks and lift our spirits. Longer days, more sun and clean light all allow us more time to indulge in maximising this uplifting month, but only if we don't fill all our time and space with 'things'. How will you use March to restore your energy, provide fresh experiences and move forward with the things that matter in all the parts of your life?

For myself and for many others, it is a time when I suddenly remember that I have financial obligations, and I need to revisit my understanding of what is happening with my money. The more I do in March, the better and less pressured my April will be. A lesson I have been slow to learn in the past. Previously in March, my accountants have been left wringing their hands in despair, waiting for the information essential for financial clarity. This rigorous preparation also can provide you with the means to savour satisfaction of a year well done, or adapt into a year in which it may, otherwise, be difficult to embark on your new financial journey.

So my primary thoughts in March centre on making financial planning and sorting my actions so that I am clear what my position is by year end. I know that one of the greatest sources of personal and relationship pressure has occurred when I've not dealt with financial concerns, and not kept up to date. The ability to have accurate financial information puts me in a strong position to deal with changes in the year ahead and respond to cash flow blips.

Whatever your financial circumstances, it is a good time to answer some key questions:

How clear are you about your current financial position?

What should you be able to understand and know about your financial affairs?

How can you put yourself in a position that enables you to make better personal and business decisions?

What financial help might you need?

If you have moving from financial confusion to business clarity as an aim throughout the month, April suddenly appears very rose tinted. So, many of your other plans will fall into place and you will stand above the scrambling detail that keeps us stuck in the present.

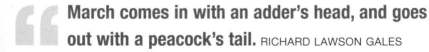

March comes in with an adder's head, and goes out with a peacock's tail. RICHARD LAWSON GALES

April

> As children, our imaginations are vibrant, and our hearts open. We believe that the bad guy always loses and that the tooth fairy sneaks into our rooms at night to put money under our pillow. Everything amazes us, and we think anything is possible. We continuously experience life with a sense of newness and unbridled curiosity. YEHUDA BERG

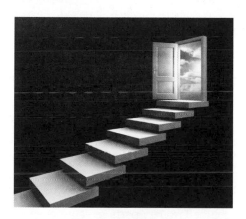

This is the month of starting afresh, clearing away clutter and cleaning up messes. It's also a period to savour growth, enjoy the changing conditions and admire the miracle of newness. If you can kick-start your 'new' year during April, you will sow the seeds for later growth and provide a strong base for the remainder of the year. Your energy store will provide the resilience you need when things get tough.

Allow some time for reflection of these questions, and use them as prompts into action and putting yourself out there:

What haven't you done for some time that would reinvigorate the important elements of your life?

What is it the right time to start, what will be the first steps towards achieving a dream, ambition or long-held desire?

What can you throw away, recycle or give away that will signal the end of a period for you and others?

Some of the things that we shut away are worth revisiting in the light of recent changes and identifying how you can maximise what you already have available. What have you stored away that needs to be re-opened, used again, revisited or repaired? What skills or experience do you have that may be under-used?

Remember that the first is April Fools' Day. This day represents jokes, hilarity, clever pranks and feasting. You can start the month by adopting a position that represents lightness of touch, laughter and shared good humour. With the pressures coming from demands at work, we all need to balance the toughness with positive thoughts and actions.

How can you contribute towards creating a more positive, fun environment where you work?

My top tips for April:

→ Open all of your windows and take in the freshness that is enveloping everything.

→ Take a trip to the recycling centre and charity shop with things you have outgrown, that are creating clutter or you have decided you no longer need. This can be a very therapeutic process.

→ Visit a local farm, particularly when children are there. Notice how you begin to smile and feel young again.

→ Clean or paint the favourite parts of your house, areas that have become a little tired or where you want to create a fresh look.

→ Plant your favourite flowers and cut the grass. Then enjoy that smell and open a bottle of New Zealand Sauvignon Blanc.

→ Get back into your favourite activity regime by committing to classes, games and sessions with others.

Of course, your office or workplace is in just as big a need of clearing and cleansing. Now is the time to clean your files from computers, ask others for their fresh ideas, involve colleagues and staff in finding the best ways of introducing different processes and systems, and encourage new thinking on issues and challenges that have remained stagnant or unresolved.

Look at ways that you can introduce fresh plants and flowers more widely into your life and work.

Reawaken your taste buds with the freshness of new-season produce eaten at the right time of year.

> **Make me over, Mother April, When the sap begins to stir! When thy flowery hand delivers, All the mountain-prisoned rivers, And thy great heart beats and quivers, to revive the days that were.** RICHARD HOVEY

May

> **Success is where preparation and opportunity meet.** BOBBY UNSER

The month often announces itself through gusts of high wind but, for many young people, it's heads down inside, in preparation for their examinations. We attach an enormous amount of importance to studying towards achieving high grades during this time and, without realising it, we can generate great pressure and allow this focus to become all-consuming.

If you have others around you who are involved in this period of preparation, how can you support them and help to reduce some of the pressure during this time? If it builds, then focus moves away from studying into displacement activity. High support with a healthy lifestyle equate to having more energy, focus, concentration and application.

From my work with sixth formers I have identified some ways that parents, family members and friends can provide the best support.

→ Remember, it's their life not yours. I encounter so many parents and family members who allow their goals and ambitions negatively to influence others, often with the best of intentions, yet are relatively unaware of the pressure they are creating. It is their schedule they need to commit to and learn to follow.

→ This is also a time to pick your battles and allow some flexibility and leeway in your expectations. Decide what is critical to maintaining your home and family as a cohesive unit throughout this time. Operate at your magnanimous best, allowing small or non-essential things to pass. Accept that behaviour and mood may fluctuate and be very different from the norm during this time of strain. Remind yourself it is not done on purpose to antagonise you.

→ Create an oasis of stillness and calm, with rooms free from clamour. Allocate places for study that are off limits to others, particularly younger siblings.

→ Provide a number of their favourite moments of pleasure, as rewards and recognition, when progress is made. These are best when they involve pampering, fun, comfortable or relaxing activities.

→ Create opportunities for them to let off steam and time for emotional discharge. If outlets are not found, the pressure resulting from suppression will build up and block learning and performance. Therefore, be available to listen, at their behest, when the strain is increasing.

→ Look for opportunities to encourage, congratulate and relieve pressure. Catch others doing things right, not making mistakes.

Powering Through Pressure

→ Consciously set out to remove blocks and barriers to their achieving success. Notice what you are doing to generate pressure for others and take actions to remove these elements.

All of these ways of making life more positive for those who are facing examinations are just as relevant for those at work or in situations that involve preparation for a major event. So, in your business, make May the month for recognising the pressure that others are facing. It's a great time of year for team away days and well-being events.

> The study and knowledge of the universe would somehow be lame and defective were no practical results to follow. MARCUS TULLIUS CICERO

June

> I'm often at events when they're quite light-hearted social events when people would want me to kid around. JOHN KEY

This is the month we associate often with the start of great popular events, pageantry, festivals and major sporting occasions. It's a time when everything around us shouts out, 'Get into the social spirit, look for new clothes, put yourself out there, girl, celebrate achievement and recognise your greatness.' However, do you listen to these messages and take advantage of the opportunities to lighten up your life?

Hopefully, the sun's warmth will remind you to look up more, smile often, immerse yourself in social occasions and find reasons why it is so good to engage with others in our favourite pursuits.

What can you do to make the most of June?

→ Look for a maximum fix of Vitamin D by allowing yourself to spend as much time as possible in the light, sensibly soaking up the rays. We need to compensate for all the time we have spent indoors and covered up.

→ Find out what is being celebrated and taking place outdoors in your area. We often take local events for granted and miss opportunities to engage with neighbours in different, positive contexts.

→ Make a point of maximising the longest days by eating outdoors, having picnics and indulging in the wonderful seasonable produce. Socialising in the evening is easier as people want to be out and about. This is the ideal time of year to engage in physical activity when you do have more light and time in the evenings.

→ Get out of your business areas as early as possible each day. If it means working in a more efficient, paced and rigorous way, find and pursue it.

→ Enjoy your new-found energy, vitality and health to push yourself to achieve more physically. Set yourself some new goals that you now know are achievable.

→ Plan your whole week around those events that meet your social, physical and recreational needs. Where do you need to put your needs first during this month?

→ Go out there to places that inspire you and make some new friends and acquaintances. It's a great time of year to combine business and social networking without it being an effort. Talk to people you do not normally notice or recognise.

→ What can you do that will signal you are embracing the warmth, light and sociability associated with June?

→ How will you use your time differently to make the most of the longer days?

→ What will make you smile more this month?

This is a great time of year to relax by letting your hair down, doing daft things, playing and indulging in social silliness. This applies just as much in our work.

" Spring being a tough act to follow, God created June. AL BERNSTEIN

July

" When adversity strikes, that's when you have to be the most calm. Take a step back, stay strong, stay grounded and press on. L. L. COOL J.

I am positively biased in favour of July, as it is filled by my cancerian spirit, coming to the fore during my birthday month. It actually falls on Bastille Day, which I have always taken as being symbolic of the desire to fight for a cause and pursue what I believe are the 'important' parts of life. I was incredibly impressed during my job review one year when my boss, half seriously, labelled me 'a bloody revolutionary'. When it comes to pursuing what you value and believe in, he was absolutely right.

What strikes me more with each increasingly rapid passing year, is the need to seize opportunities, embrace manageable risks and to fight the important battles for what you believe is important. For many of my clients, the opposite has been true for much of their lives, because they have become driven by fear, over hope.

Personal case study

I take as a typical example a client I knew well and worked with for some time, Rachel. She appeared to create continual anxiety for herself, usually by focussing on all the 'bad' news she heard. She became upset easily about 'awful' world events and focussed on what was not happening, going wrong or not getting done. When we met, she told me about many situations that suggested she saw danger around every corner and at times meant she experienced panic attacks, especially in crowds. She was fearful of her home security, seizing on every snippet of local information, often picked up by the well-intentioned neighbourhood watch.

I am a great advocate of the type of support offered by cognitive behaviour and other linked therapies. I value the practical sense involved, and I therefore used some of the techniques with Rachel over a period of time, to help reduce her anxiety levels.

First, at a macro level, where she realised that she was able to accept the 'bad' news as not being truly representative of the area in which she lived and socialised, or of the people around her.

Second, convincing herself that it was okay to ask for and get family and friend support when she embarked on certain activities, in places that might be more crowded. Talking more about positive elements, which she engineered deliberately with those frequently around her, changed some of her 'negative' focus and perspective. She also began to realise that many people had fears and anxieties like her own, and she learnt from them by discussing ways they successfully dealt with these.

Third, using alternative media, what I call the 'good news sheets', she developed a positive and curious habit for seeking examples of success and always looking for a balanced point of view and data, when she encountered things that concerned her.

Finally, introducing some new response techniques enabled her to recognise potential panic onset and gave her ways that she could affect the circumstances she was in.

These combined changes had a cumulative effect and her outlook gradually became much more positively biased and optimistic.

It is now worth you taking time to identify how your fears may be affecting elements of your life and adding pressure in situations where there are actions you can take to dramatically reduce concerns.

Activity

Ask yourself these questions:

What is something that regularly generates anxiety for me?

Specifically, in what situations does it occur? What is different about these situations?

What am I aware of in the way I respond?

How do I want to respond differently? (Think of times when you have behaved in the ways you value.)

Where will I practise this alternative?

Who will I ask to support me with this?

This is also the month where I revisit my key relationships, check out how I'm doing in pursuit of my values and attempt to create as big a celebration as possible.

How can you use this focus to pursue what is really important in life and search for ways of overcoming obstacles, as a useful checkpoint for you in July?

> **Unrest of spirit is a mark of life; one problem after another presents itself and in the solving of them we can find our greatest pleasure.** KAL MENNINGER

August

> ## To many, Heathrow in August is a paradigm of Hell. PAUL JOHNSON

This is the time of embarking on holidays and, for many people, it will either greatly restore, or deplete, their energy. Your attitude towards how you use this time will dramatically affect what you and others gain from what is an essential break or 'time out'.

Personal case study

At one point I worked with a colleague who prepared for holidays, three years in advance. By the time the holiday arrived, everything was in place and set up, to ensure a 10/10 star break. You would imagine that they had the best holidays ever, wouldn't you? Wrong! Each time they returned something had not gone according to plan, schedules had been changed, transport was delayed, and unexpected events dictated alterations to many plans. They operated their holiday strategy in ways they normally used to run a business. Of course, they never quite realised the connection to what they experienced often with work projects or the powerful influence of similar external pressure factors, which often were outside their control.

So, how can you give yourself the best chance of getting the most from your holiday time? Like anything that is important, you need to put certain things in place and adopt flexible planning to give yourself the best chance of success and not build in additional pressure from 'getting it wrong'.

Some of the best practices that have been identified as contributing to successful, energy-enhancing holidays, include:

→ adopting an attitude of 'this is my/our break', which needs to be managed selfishly and executed flexibly, to provide what you most need at that time;

→ thinking about what you and others want to do that will meet some of your needs. Talk about where you can compromise and encourage give and take, when you and others want different things. Decide on the one thing that matters most, then be prepared to negotiate over other elements. This will prevent fixed positions creating animosity, before any decisions have been taken;

→ planning the most important things to confirm or put in place, so that these confirmed arrangements will provide some security, without being claustrophobic;

→ making the most of spontaneously getting involved in whatever is happening around you. This can range from unexpected time for solitude and quiet, to discovery of noisy, colourful parades, celebrations, exhibitions, events and festivals. In this way, you will get more of your needs met, and understand more about, and enjoy, the places you are visiting;

→ planning your work well in advance of a holiday, so that you are gradually closing down as you approach D-day. Most of us are dispensable, and you will find that it does others good to have to take responsibility in your absence. Many people find themselves getting ill at the start of their holidays, often because they push themselves too hard at the last minute and their bodies realise as they relax that it is time to push all the rubbish they have built up, outwards;

→ leaving your electronic equipment at home or away from immediate access. Having mobiles and iPads at our sides puts us on alert, and it becomes much harder to relax and fully enjoy the experience with others around you. Let your families and friends at home do without you! I have found that, with planning and by informing others of my unavailability, little of importance arises whilst I am away and inaccessible;

→ travelling as lightly as possible, enabling ease of access on cheaper flights. If you need additional everyday items they will be available locally, often at low cost;

→ staying as positively focussed as possible, despite any potentially frustrating experiences. Much of the joy of experiencing other cultures comes from appreciating that they do things in different ways. This is the time to accept that things that are often outside of our control or influence do happen. When you need to resolve problems, use a firm approach and identify the right person who can take action. Sounding off aggressively at a ticketing clerk or receptionist often will worsen the situation, not deal with the issues. Find out who can help and what your options are;

→ doing what feels right and affordable for you at the time. For different people, the most pleasurable breaks come from working on the house, spending time with people in difficult circumstances, throwing yourself into wild adventures, allowing complete beach shut-downs or adventurously conquering mountains or oceans. If you like doing the same things in the same ways, great! I prefer to see different places, people and cultures. It's all about meeting our different needs and experiencing the lasting effect afterwards, when you are back at work. Still having energy, memories and enthusiasm are the real test of an excellent holiday.

Remember that the best holidays are about connecting with and celebrating your own and others' needs, desires and ambitions. They should be a recognition of jobs well done and a life at home well lived.

" Sharing the holiday with other people, and feeling that you're giving of yourself, gets you past all the commercialism. CAROLINE KENNEDY

Powering Through Pressure

September

> The actual atoms and molecules that make up my brain and body today are not the same ones that I was born with on 8 September 1954, a half-century ago this month.

MICHAEL SHERMER

I associate September with moving on, letting go and creating something different. The signals to invite this are in the air and change is again evident in every place. Moving on doesn't mean that you are giving up. It means that you are making a choice to be happy, instead of being hurt. Therefore it feels important during this month that we deal with a sense of anti-climax after holidays, make the most of constantly changing periods of sunshine and rain, enjoy spurts of social activity and put in periods of hard work to catch up.

Personal case study

The need to have this September positivity really struck me when I worked with Tom, who was approaching retirement. He had poured an enormous amount ▶

of himself into his work, in fact he stated, 'My work is my life.' His partner had passed away unexpectedly two years before, and he was finding it difficult to reconcile not having a focus and purpose, at a time when he was still very much on his own. September, also being the anniversary of his wife's death, 'always produced bouts of sadness, regret and loneliness'. In fact, these feelings were accompanied by signs of heart and blood pressure issues, which appeared to be absolutely linked to his mental and emotional state.

Our work did not produce miraculous changes. Loss, regret and fear of an uncertain future often take considerable personal work and ongoing support over time to affect these states. What he did achieve was the generation of a new focus around bowls and allotment gardening, where he encountered and spent time with others, some of whom were in similar positions. He made a conscious choice to retire slightly early, which generated financial security and created an opportunity to embark on new experiences, particularly treating himself to a cruise each September. Most importantly, he started to have regular conversations with his wife and he developed positive rituals of remembrance.

Dealing with his personal circumstances in a fresh way helped him to deal with his work losses and he found new enjoyable activities to immerse himself in. For Tom, September was no longer the dark month he once dreaded.

We can also associate with this experience where we connect certain times of the year with negative feelings. The same thing applies to how we perceive loss in personal relationships and friendships.

Consider this time as one when you can examine how you deal with difficult and potentially conflicting feelings.

Is there a time of year that you associate with loss, regret or loneliness?

What have you done to make this time one of rightful remembrance but not darkness?

What did you do to let go? Are there things you still need to find a way out of?

Is there a message from this about other emotionally charged periods of your life?

In what ways can you dedicate September to positively remember, let go and move on for things that have happened in the previous year or eight months?

Powering Through Pressure

As we go through change almost always there will be a sense of some loss or memory of good times. What is essential is that this looking to the past does not become the driving force for what is happening to you in the present or stop you moving forward in the future. Sometimes we need to develop rituals that signify that we have let go. I remember how critical it was at the end of a turbulent relationship to ensure that things that belonged to my ex-partner were given back, at the right time. At work, the same applies to changing jobs, where it helps to take the best of what you have learnt into a new role without holding on to the elements of your previous one, when they may no longer serve a purpose.

As much as September represents the onset of autumn, it also signifies a fading of elements in our life that we no longer have or perhaps need to hold onto.

It also represents storing up for the winter and conserving what is of most value.

> ## I did a concert ... in September with the Berlin Philharmonic ... They're great musicians, and there's always something to learn from them. CECILIA BARTOLI

This period also represents a period of consolidation and learning, which will stand you in good stead for the times ahead. What have you learnt during the enlightenment of spring and summer that will help you through the rest of the year?

Consider what you need to visit, conserve, put in place or lay down to protect your health and well-being over the next six months.

> ## My favourite poem is the one that starts 'Thirty days hath September' because it actually tells you something. GROUCHO MARX

October

October is the fallen leaf, but it is also a wider horizon more clearly seen. It is the distant hills once more in sight, and the enduring constellations above them once again. HAL BORLAND

The days seem to be quickly shortening, the winds often get stronger and we can become consumed by the gripping onset of Seasonal Affective Disorder (SAD). I believe that all of us experience mood changes, less energy and vulnerability to illness, as a result of the seasonal changes we experience most in October. Look around you and notice how busy people are, how little time there is to stop and talk, and how tired and emotional others appear.

This is the time to take action before SAD takes hold and your physical and mental states shrink in on themselves. Think about which of the following ideas you can adopt now, so that you will put a strong foundation in place for the whole winter. It is just as important for you to lay in your stock as protection. Also think about the extent to which you and others can talk yourselves into a potentially weakened state of decline or a fired-up resilient state.

A good place to start involves accepting some of the truths about being in October, with the winter ahead.

→ It is only eight months until the longest day. Shorter days can sometimes encourage us to do more, stay focussed and be more productive.

→ The coolness enables us to feel more comfortable exercising and doing other activities. The numbers in most classes start to rise at this time, creating more of an atmosphere and bringing a greater vital energy.

→ It's a great time to book up to see theatre, movies, dance, gigs, etc. Tickets for the summer festivals soon will be on sale and you can plan for Glastonbury, Isle of Wight, Leeds.

→ Winter food provides a wholesome diet and the minerals we need to protect our immune systems. Set up some dinner evenings, which you can look forward to, demonstrate your culinary skills and immerse yourself in the planning.

→ Darkness in the evenings provides us with a great excuse to leave work earlier and enables us to travel in greater safety. Get out of the door now!

→ Guinness, red wine and real ale taste wonderful and generally are the more healthy alcoholic drinks. Mulled wine becomes acceptable, pubs have a social energy and you might even want to socialise more with colleagues.

→ It's a chance to, appropriately, get out the UGG boots and your favourite headgear.

→ You now have an excuse to curl up in front of the fire, catch up with those long-saved programmes or your favourite boxed set, stay in your PJs all day at the weekend, remain in bed longer, etc.

→ Remember, weather is only weather, it does not hold an emotional state. We impose that onto our perception of the time of year and what it represents. Do you look down and see the dirt or up and see the clear skies?

Do you need any more convincing? This is the time of year that brings warmth, closeness, wonderful contrasts and an opportunity that involves greater enjoyment of our homes.

> Long afterward, many would remember those two days in the first week of October with vividness and anguish. ARTHUR HAILEY

November

> The ingredients of both darkness and light are equally present in all of us ... the madness of this planet is largely a result of the human being's difficulty in coming to virtuous balance with himself. ELIZABETH GILBERT

We have just got over Halloween and along comes Guy Fawkes Night. What a ridiculous time of year for Guy Fawkes and his chums to attempt to set fire to the Houses of Parliament! After all, November is a time of enveloping darkness, cold, wet and wind and rarely seeing our neighbours in the streets. Perhaps it was ideal timing, if you add the fog of London during that time.

What a contrast, given what we encounter at the end of October and beginning of November, that offers a very different celebratory spirit. Two festivals that pick people up, generate fun, laughter and excitement, and allow communities to indulge in playful skulduggery together. This comes at a time when it is easy for us to shut ourselves away and become less aware of what is happening to those around us.

What are the messages of Halloween and Guy Fawkes Night? Is it the excitement and vitality of the bonfires and firework displays? Is it epitomised by the dress-up naughtiness and scaremongering of trick or treat?

For many, what strikes a chord is the unstated permission to indulge our darker side in a way that creates goodwill. Taking on roles and playing these out, in a reasonably safe environment, can be a great outlet at a time when many people appear emotionally tightly strung.

What this time suggests to me is that this is a reminder for us to look at the blend of activity that we seek, and struggle to achieve, in the different roles we take on across our lives. There have been many missives claiming success in ways of establishing work/life balance. I've often thought about the validity of 'balance' and discovered in my own and clients' experience that this can prove an almost impossible thing to achieve.

So, November can be a time for you to reflect on the important roles you have, where you have the blend or mix right and where you experience a gap that creates a pressure for you. Before you put on your devil's mask, witch's hat or set alight your candles, take some time to consider ways of getting the blend right for you between your various roles and activities.

Take each of your roles within your family, workplace and social/group environment.

Draw yourself a pie chart, which shows the amount of time and energy you devote to these roles.

Rate each of your roles in terms of your current satisfaction and positive feelings e.g. 1 = unhappy and frustrated, 10 = overjoyed and fulfilled.

Consider where you would, ideally, like to devote more time and energy.

Decide how you could develop yourself within each of these roles.

What would your ideal blend pie chart look like?

What will you need to do differently?

There are three things that I've discovered and believe will help you to generate the right blend:

→ Your blend is unique, not copied nor what others tell you to do.
→ You will need to flex your blend regularly and be prepared to have short periods that are not in perfect balance, but they are the right thing to focus your energy on at that particular point.
→ The best blend means meeting your needs as much as meeting the needs of others.

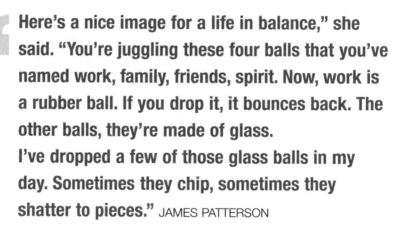

**Here's a nice image for a life in balance," she said. "You're juggling these four balls that you've named work, family, friends, spirit. Now, work is a rubber ball. If you drop it, it bounces back. The other balls, they're made of glass.
I've dropped a few of those glass balls in my day. Sometimes they chip, sometimes they shatter to pieces."** JAMES PATTERSON

December

I imagine that, for many of you, most of December is taken up worrying about ways that you can stay sane and keep well throughout Christmas time. In the frenetic run-up to Christmas it is so easy to feel overwhelmed, experience over-tiredness and face losing it emotionally.

Personal case study

When I met Rick, an IT consultant, shortly after Christmas one year, he swore he would never again allow himself to get involved in a Christmas like the one he had just experienced. Relatively newly married, he and his partner at first agreed to spend Christmas day with his in-laws and, at this point, the battle started. They spent weeks changing arrangements and attempting to pacify and deal with the negative, emotionally loaded behaviour of his parents. The plan they finally agreed meant that throughout the Christmas break they had to travel virtually the length of the UK, in fact, spending more time on trains and at stations and in motorway services than celebrating. He had worked long hours in the week leading up to Christmas Eve and was on call for part of the Christmas period.

▶

One of the results of the frenetic activity, and resultant wear-and-tear, was his succumbing to a bout of influenza, starting on Boxing Day. Food poisoning on New Year's Eve capped a disastrous week for his health and general state.

In amongst this chaos, he forgot to look early enough to buy a special online present for his wife. By the time it arrived on 28 December he was really in the dog house. To cap it off, in their hurry to leave their newly furnished house, he left the keys in the front door and they were burgled whilst away from home.

From our work together, at the beginning of the following year, Rick kept to his word and generally changed his work pattern, reducing the level of his commitments and absolutely including time with his wife, on their own, during Christmas Day, when the next festive season arrived.

You may recognise elements of this scenario. The good news is that you can start doing things throughout the autumn and this month to help you to remain calmer, have more energy and really enjoy this time of year.

Here are my top 10 tips:

1   It is essential to pace yourself throughout the holiday period. It is easy to have mad bursts of activity and socialising that leave you feeling drained of energy and enthusiasm. Plan to spread your celebrations, so that you get rest time between activities and can enjoy the sociable elements throughout this period even more.

2   Find some space for yourself to enjoy quietness or have a place to go to where you can do your favourite on-your-own activities. Technology has made this easier to do, so take advantage of others wanting to test out their iPads.

3   Balance your needs and the demands of others. These often get compromised in the clamour to please everyone, resulting in no one being satisfied. You do not have to see everyone on Christmas Day and Boxing Day. Make decisions that may mean some negotiation of arrangements, to ensure you get more of what you want. Spreading visits, family events and social occasions throughout December and into early January is a great way of avoiding over-commitment and making the most of Christmas-time.

4 Be canny about shopping. All of the shops are open long hours, so avoid peak times. I have made it a practice to go only to my favourite places and particularly to support small, local businesses. An early spurt of online activity for other purchases, on a wet Sunday early in December, solves many problems.

5 Give yourself relaxing treats and presents to counter-balance any high periods of activity that feel hectic and leave you feeling frustrated or upset. The right means of pampering yourself and others is essential during this time.

6 Do a lot of your favourite things and spend more time with the people who enrich you. Catch yourself starting to feel on edge and, at that point, contact or meet with friends and family who make you laugh, take you away from the shopping frenzy and are fun to relax or play with. At the least arrange three of these life-saving time slots, strategically placed to compensate for any feelings of over-kill.

7 Allow some of the family 'stuff' and fluctuating moods of your co-workers to flow over your head, so it isn't taken personally. Spend more of your contact time listening, observing and paying attention to others. You may be surprised what happens when you stay quiet or play a low-key role. If you have always done it, let others take the lead and shoulder more of the workload.

8 Eat and drink only what you know is the right amount for you. Balance any over-eating with more activities that will burn off those extra calories and re-energise you. Many people find it useful to have a period before Christmas where their intake of rich food, fats, sugars and carbohydrates is markedly reduced.

9 Get out into the light as much as possible, enjoy natural things and walk or cycle whenever you can, rather than drive. Top up your diet with immune-boosting supplements, particularly zinc and vitamins C and D.

10 Remember that Christmas can be a delightful time without spending a lot of money and overdoing the entertainment. Remind yourself that many kids spend more time playing with their boxes than the presents you spent a fortune on. People love you for who you are and not what you buy for them!

Remind yourself what Christmas time is about and invest some time in others, those you may have lost contact with, have forgotten, are lonely or have not been seen for a while. Think about people who are not in as fortunate a position as you are, and take action to help make their Christmas a better time. Supporting local charities or volunteering can lift others' spirits and your own.

> **I have always thought of Christmas time, when it has come round, as a good time; a kind, forgiving, charitable time; the only time I know of, in the long calendar of the year, when men and women seem by one consent to open their shut-up hearts freely, and to think of people below them as if they really were fellow passengers to the grave, and not another race of creatures bound on other journeys.** CHARLES DICKENS

Now it's your turn

> **All the suffering, stress and addiction comes from not realising you already are what you are looking for.** JON KABAT-ZINN

I hope that this book has taken you on a journey that has guided you to be more aware of your state, to understand your role in situations that generate pressure, and to develop a range of stress preventers.

Whilst you have fresh ideas for taking care of yourself, I recommend that you assess where you are with my favourite top 10 ideas and commit to using those that will make the biggest difference in your life and work.

1 For any important activity, decide what you want to achieve and focus on that.

2 Consider fresh ways of learning by undertaking different types of experiences.

3 Slow down, breathe and pause whenever it feels like the treadmill is speeding up.

4 You need the right people on your radar, and want to be on theirs.

5 Give your time and energy to others and they will support you when you need help.

6 Get feedback from the people who matter, understand what it means for you, then act.

7 Whenever demands are being made on you by others, be prepared to negotiate over what is possible.

8 Seek out positive, energising people and celebrate success with them on a regular basis.

9 Value and appreciate how good you are already and play to your strengths.

10 Do something **now**.

I hope that my personal sense of what each month can be about will help you to find ways of building strength, energy and resilience to stop stress in its tracks on a regular basis.

So, much good luck and success in your quest to build resilience, manage pressure and stop stress.

> **The greatest weapon against stress is our ability to choose one thought over another.** WILLIAM JAMES

Who is out there to help you?

It is always useful to know who is available to turn to when we are facing issues that may be generating pressure for ourselves and others.

These are some of the known and recognised organisations that are involved directly in stress, pressure at work, and mental health issues and support.

ACAS

Helpline: 08457 474 747

Website: www.acas.org.uk

Provides online advice in a number of areas of improving health, work and well-being. This includes stress, promoting positive mental health, fitness for work and employee engagement.

Anxiety Care UK

Tel: 07552 877 219

Website: www.anxietycare.org.uk

Helps people suffering from anxiety disorders to plan, initiate and carry through their own recovery programmes. Deals especially with phobias and obsessive compulsive disorders.

Anxiety UK

Tel: 08444 775 774

Website: www.anxietyuk.org.uk

Supports those living with anxiety disorders by providing information, support and understanding via an extensive range of services, including 1:1 therapy.

British Association for Behavioural and Cognitive Psychotherapies (BABCP)

Tel: 0161 705 4304

Website: www.babcp.com

Provides research and accreditation of therapists who provide behavioural and cognitive therapies. Focusses particularly on anxiety, bereavement and depression.

British Association for Counselling and Psychotherapy (BACP)

Tel: 01455 883 300

Website: www.itsgoodtotalk.org.uk

Provides information about counselling and therapy, including details of local practitioners who support people to deal with difficulties and make positive changes.

The British Psychological Society (BPS)

Tel: 0116 254 9568

Website: www.bps.org.uk

Produces a directory of, and trains, chartered psychologists.

Citizens Advice

Advice line tels: 08444 111 444 (England); 08444 772 020 (Wales)

TextRelay service: 08444 111 445

Website: www.citizensadvice.org.uk with online advice from www.advice guide.org.uk

Provides initial, confidential advice on a wide range of issues, including employment problems.

The Complementary Medical Association (CMA)

Tel: 0845 129 8434

Website: www.the-cma.org.uk

Has a register of professional practitioners and training courses. CMA helps the public and doctors to realise that complementary and integrative medicine is – when delivered safely and ethically – a viable and highly desirable form of healthcare.

Employment Tribunal Guidance

Tel: 0845 795 9775

Website: www.justice.gov.uk/tribunals/employment

Gives guidance on the tribunal system. This can generate pressure for people going through a tribunal process and hearings.

Equality and Human Rights Commission

Equality Advisory Support Service tel: 0808 800 0082

Textphone: 0808 800 0084

Website: www.equalityhumanrights.com

Information and advice on equality and rights issues that involve discrimination. Its aim is to promote equality across the nine 'protected' grounds – age, disability, gender, race, religion and belief, pregnancy and maternity, marriage and civil partnership, sexual orientation and gender reassignment.

GOV.UK

Website: www.gov.uk/browse/benefits

Information about employment rights, specific benefits and help for disability, and work injury and accident.

Health and Safety Executive

Website: www.hse.gov.uk

The national independent watchdog for work-related health, safety and illness. Provides organisations with assessments to measure compliance with health and safety legislation.

ISMA (International Stress Management Association)

Website: www.isma.org.uk

Tel: 0845 680 7083 or 01292 423391

Email: stress@isma.org.uk

Central governing body for standards and quality in dealing with stress, managing pressure and building resilience. Maintains an up-to-date register of practitioners.

Jobcentre plus

Website: www.gov.uk/contact-jobcentre-plus

For help with finding a job, making claims and being retrained.

Mind

Mind Infoline: 0300 123 3393

Website: www.mind.org.uk

Email: info@mind.org.uk

To ensure that anyone with a mental health problem has somewhere to turn for advice and support. A language line is available for talking in a language other than English.

Mindfulness-based Cognitive Therapy

Website: www.mbct.co.uk

Information about the therapy, classes in mindfulness and training. Specifically supporting people who are experiencing repeated bouts of depression.

NICE (National Institute for Health and Care Excellence)

Website: www.nice.org.uk

Information and guidelines on recommended treatments for a wide range of health disorders.

No Panic (National Organisation for Phobias, Anxiety, Neurosis, Information and Care)

Helpline: 0800 138 8889

Website: www.nopanic.org.uk

Provides a helpline, practical step-by-step programmes and ongoing support for those with anxiety disorders.

Samaritans

24-hour helpline: 08457 909 090

Email: jo@samaritans.org

Website: www.samaritans.org

Emotional support for anyone feeling down or struggling to cope who needs a first port of call or listening ear.

The Stress Management Society

Tel: 020 3142 8650

Website: www.stress.org.uk

A non-profit-making organisation dedicated to providing training and information that will help people to tackle stress.

SupportLine

Helpline tel: 01708 765 200

Website: www.supportline.org.uk

Offers confidential emotional support to children, young adults and adults by telephone, email and post. The Helpline is primarily a preventative service and aims to support people before they reach the point of crisis. It is aimed particularly at those who are socially isolated, the vulnerable, at-risk groups and victims of any form of abuse.

UK Council for Psychotherapy (UKCP)

Tel: 020 7014 9955

Website: www.psychotherapy.org.uk

A membership organisation with a voluntary register of qualified psychotherapists with an emphasis on supporting children and young people.

The Work Foundation

Website: www.theworkfoundation.com

Independent foundation looking at work issues and policy improvement for the benefit of society.

Working Families

Tel: 0300 012 0312

Website: www.workingfamilies.org.uk

Information for working parents and carers on achieving work-life balance when faced by complex demands.

Index